Expert Praise

"Darren Kelly has written a book that can serve as a mentor to anyone interested in succeeding. HELLO PROFIT is clear, concise, and proves that Darren is a dedicated teacher. A job well done!"

Donald J. Trump

"Everybody needs to reinvent themselves at some point in their life. I believe Darren's book will help people discover their hidden talents and open their minds up to new challenges. It has a lot more to offer than just how to put the WOW into sales! You won't be disappointed."

Dermot Desmond
International Investment & Underwriting
Owner, Celtic Football Club

"This incredible book is loaded with valuable insight and practical ideas to increase your sales immediately!"

Brian Tracy
The world's most successful sales author
The Psychology of Selling

*"The chapter on negotiating
in this great book
is well worth the price of the book."*

Roger Dawson
America's Premier Business Negotiator
Author, Secrets of Power Negotiating

*"An enlightening book
for success in sales and life."*

Allan and Barbara Pease
The world's best known communication authors
The Definitive Book on Body Language

*"Too many marketing people
focus on entertaining their prospects
rather than selling to them.
Darren Kelly sets them straight
with his inspiring new book
which is also a joy to read."*

Al Ries
Co-creator of the marketing term 'positioning'
Co-Author, The Origin of Brands

*"In today's tough trading place
your proposition to client
has to differentiate itself;
it needs a WOW factor.
Darren Kelly shows how quality,
value, and innovation
will put your business
on the right track."*

**Lawrence Tomlinson
Chairman, LNT Group
British Government Business Adviser**

*"Darren's genius is his language:
short, interesting sentences set a pace
which keeps you reading and before
you know it you are fifty pages in
and have learnt something."*

**Sarah Day
Managing Partner, DLA Piper UK LLP (Leeds)**

*"HELLO PROFIT shows you numerous ways
to WOW every customer
and win more business."*

**Jill Konrath
Author, SNAP Selling**

*"Forget about 'the hard sell'
and 'the soft sell'.
There's only one way to sell.
Sell with WOW."*

Darren Kelly

HELLO PROFIT

Outsell & Outnegotiate
everyone with WOW

DARREN KELLY

Copyright © 2013 **Darren Kelly**
All rights reserved. See back of book for conditions.
Printed by Nerrad Books

ISBN: 1492815497
ISBN 13: 9781492815495

Dedication

I dedicate this book to my late and loving dad, Brendan. When the building trade collapsed in the eighties in Ireland, he worked in a clothes factory. When the factory went on three day weeks, he dug graves to pay the bills. When he had no money to fix his car, he walked to the graveyard with his shovel. Profit to him was a good thing.

Profit makes a company solid and productive. It helps it innovate and grow. It helps a company create jobs. It helps people in those jobs pay their way, contribute to society, and grow. When my dad stood knee deep in a freshly dug grave, he prayed for profit: he had seven children to feed.

This Powerful & easy-to-use Toolkit

will help you achieve

- ☐ greater confidence
- ☐ greater focus
- ☐ faster sales
- ☐ faster repeat sales
- ☐ increased transaction sizes
- ☐ greater cross and up-selling success
- ☐ increased customer retention
- ☐ superior product and service launches
- ☐ profitable strategic partnerships
- ☐ elevated market share
- ☐ better cash flow
- ☐ higher profit margins
- ☐ and much more

About Darren

Educated at the Dublin Institute of Technology, Darren Kelly's exceptional experiences and studies offer you the ultimate edge.

A proven sales and motivation coach: 3 iTunes #1 audio-books. Companies seek his coaching and consultancy for sales, media relations, presentations, and personal excellence. Building relationships that create an authentic contribution for a better world lie at the heart of his work

A trusted media expert: ex-radio personality on Heart FM, Smooth Radio, Real Radio, and a regular guest on BBC Radio. As a Heart FM radio personality, he was trusted by the world's biggest record companies to interview and promote artists such as George Michael, Cher, Duran Duran, Ricky Martin, UB40, and Lionel Richie. In 2005, Disney said they were blown away by his live broadcast from Florida.

A credible subject matter expert: studied over 2,000 books, articles, and whitepapers, and advised everyone from sales teams at small companies to lawyers at leading global law firms. Kelly has also interviewed key leaders on the Forbes and Sunday Times Rich lists.

An entertainer: as the host of the Buy Yorkshire Conference (North of England's biggest B2B Conference) he brings a mix of passion, energy, fun, and focus.

Contents

Foreword xv
Profit, Selling, WOW, & One xvii
WOW Results xix

Part 1. 1

1. Gratitude for Growth 3
2. Values for Victory 25
3. Energy for Excellence 41
4. Listening for Luck 61
5. Sharing for Success 77
6. Network for Net Worth 95

Part 2. 117

7. Belief for Brilliance 119
8. Rapport for Relationships 143
9. Wisdom for Winning 169
10. Passion for Promotion 183
11. Habit for Harmony 213

Part 3. 225

12. Asking for Agreement · 227
13. Nerve for Negotiation · 239
14. Time for Triumph · 259
15. Caution for Crises · 275
WOW Forever · 301

Index · 327

Foreword

As the founder of DFS (UK and Ireland) and the Trustee Chairman of the Duke of Edinburgh's Award I understand the challenges of serving, supporting, and succeeding in business and life.

Whether you are selling products and services or a vision for a better world, it's essential to create and communicate benefits and value. Your competition will invariably make claims to be better, faster, cheaper, and more caring than you. Consequently it's vital to move to the next level and create a feeling of WOW in the minds of the people you serve and support.

Benjamin Disraeli famously said, "The secret of success is to be ready when your opportunity comes." This indispensable guide helps make you ready – more than a book, it's your mentor.

Darren's insight, depth of knowledge and passion for the art and science of authentic selling are profound. His great respect for the opportunity he has been given to teach and inspire people to develop confidence and skill and to communicate their value is palpable on every page.

If you want to outsell and out negotiate your competition, you must read this book.

Per Laborem ad Honorem (from labour to honour) - My old school motto.

Lord Kirkham

Profit, Selling, WOW, & One

Profit is the money that exists after total expenses are deducted from total sales.

Selling is the trustworthy transfer of a valuable product, service, or idea to today's customer in exchange for a fair price.

WOW is the spiritual, emotional, and intellectual desire to serve today's customer. It thrills, excites, and amazes them. Their whisper or roar of WOW offers a lifetime promise of profit.

One-Win is a relationship that benefits all parties and serves the global community.

One-Company is a group of people who create an enriching work environment and WOW customer experiences through their communications.

WOW Results

"WOW places you and your products and services in the number one spot in today's customer's heart."

Darren Kelly

- ☐ WOW - The Key to Success
- ☐ The Art of WOW
- ☐ Inside Your Competition
- ☐ Inside Today's Customer
- ☐ You're the Brand

WOW - The Key to Success

This is an exciting time for you because your sales IQ is about to be transformed with WOW. Make no mistake about it. You need WOW. Why? Because selling is the most visible factor that influences your personal and professional success. You only make money or advance an idea when you

- sell to a new customer.

- up-sell a current customer.

- increase the number of times you sell to a current customer.

- develop strategic partnerships with trusted and qualified people who can sell for you.

- sell your position in a negotiation.

- sell your character, personality, and skillset.

You can't even borrow money in business unless you can sell your ability to put the money to profitable use and repay it.

The famous 19th Century author Robert Louis Stevenson said, "Everyone lives by selling something." Stevenson, the author of *The Strange Case of Dr Jekyll and Mr Hyde* would probably smile at how split personalities exist in business today. He would be intrigued by the people who exchange visions, products, and services for money, but still claim they're not in sales. He would also be astounded by the number of people and companies who neglect and underestimate the significance of selling. This book is called HELLO PROFIT for one reason: profit offers you the freedom to fulfil your destiny and your company's vision for growth. When you learn how to sell with WOW you'll be able to say 'hello' to the earnings, cost reductions, and growth opportunities that are right under your nose. WOW places you and your products and services in the number one spot in today's customer's heart. After all, when you offer irresistible value you take one step closer to becoming invaluable. You need WOW because selling in today's ultra-connected and hyper-aware world is harder than ever before. The old days of building a personal and company brand by image alone are long gone. If you inflate today's customer's expectations, but you let them down through incompetence or disrespectful communication their misery can circle your community and the world in a second.

I always know when a salesperson sells with WOW. They embrace the kind of philosophy that transformed Apple from being a computer company to being a company that connected their customer base with their deepest passions and dearest relationships. It's the kind of philosophy that Barack Obama used when he ran for president in 2008. Never before had we seen a politician engage his audience through email marketing, YouTube, Facebook, and Twitter. Obama created WOW by going to where his voters communicated, finding out what they wanted, and then he communicated his value in their language. It's the kind of philosophy that made fans of Coke smile. Think about Coke's *Share a Coke* campaign - the iconic Coke label was replaced with today's customer's name. This was genius. What did it say? You can be on the world's biggest drink brand, and you can show you care for someone else by buying them a drink with their name on it too. When you share Coke's, "moment of happiness," it makes you feel fabulous, and Coke sells more drinks. This campaign integrated social brand engagement and physical selling. Some buyers became more obsessed with finding their name on a Coke bottle than satisfying their thirst, or worrying about the calories. The lesson from this campaign is clear. Coke created an enriching experience that matched today's customer's desires. It proved that Coke's main product isn't a soft drink. Its main product is happy refreshment.

What happens if what you sell isn't a beautiful Apple product, the American dream, or the soft drink that Santa loves? What happens if you sell commonplace products and services like waste removal, legal services, accountancy, finance, paint, cars, insurance, windows, food etc.? Can you still sell with WOW? You can if you learn how to create, communicate, and deliver an enriching experience for today's customer.

This book is going to take you into the customer centred mind-set of many different businesses and professions. It's packed with over 500 insights and strategies that will help you now and forever. It's crucial for you to adopt or at least adapt the skills and strategies that work outside your profession – just like Obama did. Your next success may be inspired by a piece of magic from another industry.

Let me explain the customer-centred approach of WOW in the music industry. George Michael sat before me in 2004. The former Wham star had sung with Mary J. Blige, Whitney Houston, Elton John, Aretha Franklin, and Sir Paul McCartney. Why had he granted me this interview? Did he seriously need my help to sell his album *Patience*? His catalogue that includes the hit albums *Faith*, *Listen without Prejudice*, and *Older* had cemented his reputation as a musical star. However, Michael knew that previous performances and current awareness can't ensure current and future success. He knew that great products don't sell themselves. He also knew that you must connect with people if you want to serve them. Was Michael selling his album by talking to me? Yes, he was. He educated me on how he wrote it.

He told me that before he started to write the upbeat song *Amazing* he asked himself how he could encourage his fans to tap their feet in the first ten seconds. That's an example of WOW – engaging today's customer with a product that excites them. This megastar with a massive fan base and worldwide publicity understood that a great product never sells itself.

Let me explain the WOW philosophy of another George. George Foreman's name means different things to different generations. He's the man who sold over the 100 million Lean Mean Fat Reducing Grilling Machines to one generation, and the former two-time World Heavyweight Boxing Champion to another. He said, "If you learn to sell, it's worth more than a degree." Foreman shows us that every person on the planet, from the poorest to the richest must learn how to sell to survive and thrive. He also demonstrates that selling with WOW means being adaptable and creative towards the needs and wants of a market before engaging it with irresistible value.

But wait; there's another George who sells with WOW. George Clooney, the Hollywood actor, was interviewed by James Lipton on *Inside the Actors Studio* in 2012. He referred to everyone in the audience as "salesmen." Clooney knows a lot about selling. He sold shoes in a department store aged 18. I too sold shoes aged 18. I know that you must measure a person's feet before you offer them the shoes they desire. There's no point offering them a killer pair of shoes and then telling them you haven't got their size. To paraphrase the late trial lawyer Johnny Cochrane, 'If the shoe doesn't fit you might as well quit.' I'm not saying that you shouldn't know everything about the quality of leather, fashion trends, and who else wears the shoes. These things are essential. All I'm saying is that you must discover today's customer's needs and wants in relation to what serves them best. What's the point in offering a fabulous pair of shoes to tennis ace Maria Sharapova who's a size 10, but discovering they'd only fit

Hollywood star Eva Longoria's size 6.5 feet? It doesn't matter how much Sharapova loves the shoes she's not going to buy them. The skills Clooney learnt selling shoes have helped him sell himself to movie agents; helped him sell his movies on talk shows, and helped him sell coffee and other products in his advertising work. He also uses his excellent selling and negotiation skills to promote moral and social values as a U.N. messenger of peace.

The Art of WOW

Many people think they can sell with WOW, but their results tell a different story. We know that just because a person can speak doesn't mean they'll win an Oscar. We also know that just because a person can type doesn't mean they'll win The Nobel Prize in Literature. And just because a person can speak and type doesn't mean they'll succeed in selling their products, services, and ideas.

Just ask

- ☐ the salesperson who missed his targets for two consecutive quarters.

- ☐ the sacked leader who wasn't understood, believed, or accepted by his stakeholders.

- ☐ the bankrupt entrepreneur who couldn't persuade investors to finance her project.

- ☐ the redundant lawyer who couldn't communicate his firm's value proposition.

- ☐ the unemployed mother who lost her house because she couldn't sell her accomplishments at a job interview.

Some of these people convinced themselves that they couldn't sell, and others convinced themselves that they didn't need to sell. Some of these people believed that selling was beneath them. How wrong were they? Today's customer needs to be engaged, educated, and convinced with respect before they move to action.

This book will help you sell with WOW by using your authenticity and unique genius. It doesn't advocate spin, but it glorifies WOW. It encourages the truth to be told originally, intellectually, and emotionally alongside an obsessive desire to create value for today's customer. The rewards for this form of selling are spectacular, but you must first understand the challenges in today's over communicated world.

Inside Your Competition

Every morning, you meet close to 100 marketing messages before you leave your home. The words and logos on your toothpaste, toothbrush, shampoo, clothing, and cereal, and the contents of your fridge beg for your attention. Your newspaper, radio, mobile phone, and online accounts scream messages that hope to persuade you to buy something. How about the people who use social media to disguise their sales messages for you? You also face many more messages beyond your front door. If you live in a city, you can easily reach close to 5,000 messages before every day is over. They can include a sticker in your neighbour's car window, or a poster on a train. They can include a telesales call, the morning post, or a billboard that steals your attention from driving. They can also include advertisements and product placements on the TV you watch.

In the movie *Skyfall,* James Bond had to compete for viewer attention with the brand images of BMW, Coke, Heineken, Sony, and Omega watches. Even Tom Cruise's face in the movie *Top Gun* had to compete with Aviator sunglasses. Have you seen the movie *Castaway*? Did you really think Tom Hanks had the lead role? Surely you saw the moment a FedEx cargo plane and a FedEx truck dominated the screen when Hanks' character, Chuck Noland, a FedEx employee said goodbye to his partner played by Helen Hunt. Even Hunt had to accept that her role was usurped by a Wilson Sports bag and volleyball after the plane crash. Hanks dismissed the bag, but he placed his bloodied hand on the volleyball, created a face, and called it Wilson. You can buy a replica version online. It's the "ultimate true friend" for any volleyball player according to Wilson.

You may say that product or service placements on TV and movie screens have no effect on you. But you must ask why Heineken paid $45 million for 007 to sip their beer. Maybe you've never bought the brand names I mentioned, but there's a big possibility that your car, favourite drink, computer appliance, and fashion accessories may have played starring roles in your favourite TV programme or movie.

The truth is that someone is trying to sell you something every minute of every day. The same is also true for today's customer. They didn't wake up this morning wondering whether your day will be a happy one or not. Instead, they woke up with a list of challenges they need to address and jobs they must complete. They'll also be bombarded with sales messages. Can you blame them for making their buying decisions based on their preconceived beliefs, their friend's opinions, and their memories of their experiences? Your biggest competition may not be your business competitor. It may be the multitude of sales messages today's customer faces elsewhere. In truth, you're competing for space in their mind. To be effective, your interaction must create a WOW experience.

> "Does today's customer trust you?
> I mean; trust your skill,
> trust your communication,
> and trust you'll deliver."
>
> **Darren Kelly**

Inside Today's Customer

I use the words *today's customer* a lot in this book. I use the word *today's* because today's customer isn't like yesterday's customer. The days of debt fuelled frivolous spending are long gone. Many people and companies have very little room to maneuverer in their spending plans. So please say goodbye to their blind loyalty and their acceptance of bogus bargains and mediocre value. Don't think for one minute that just because today's customer praises you or has your loyalty card that they don't have relationships with your competitors too. In fact, I suggest you use the words *today's customer* every day of your business life. Ask yourself what it is they need and want today and tomorrow. Their habits and tastes are always evolving, so your strategy must evolve too. I use the word *customer* to include patron, guest, end user, consumer, or client. I avoid the plural for one main reason: you may communicate with the masses to sell your products and services, but you must do it as if you're offering every customer a specialised and personalised value.

Today's customer adores and demands a unique and authentic personal touch: that's why this book is needed more than ever. The misselling of numerous products and services has placed trust on the floor, and today's customer perceives that a salesperson's skill is learnt from a greed and incompetence manual. I can understand their suspicions and cynicisms. They may have suffered a salesperson who didn't listen effectively, who didn't follow up on a promise, or who didn't offer meaningful solutions for their issues. They may have suffered a salesperson who didn't try to understand them and their business, or one who misrepresented the facts. Experts in the advertising industry understand WOW. They know an advertisement must inspire today's customer to connect with your products and services to

- ☐ Appreciate them.

- ☐ Desire them.

- ☐ Value them.

- ☐ Enthuse about them.

- ☐ Respect you.

- ☐ Trust you.

- ☐ Invite you to serve them.

- ☐ Salivate over your service.

- ☐ Execute your advice to take action – buy them.

In other words, it must expose and engage to create a climate of trust and value. If you think trust is nonsense, think about this. When you win trust you get faster agreements, and this leads to lower costs and higher profits. It also increases the likelihood of turning one transaction into a lifetime customer. You do your own maths. You'll soon realise that if cash is king, then trust is the heir to the throne. Think about trust this way. If your word is worth nothing – what are you worth? Did you know that Warren Buffet once concluded a deal with Wal-Mart after a two-hour meeting? With no due diligence, the $23 billion McLane deal was settled 29 days later. Why? Trust is the simple answer. I'm not advocating quick agreements to avoid the cost of due diligence. I'm just highlighting the fact that when trust exists, profits go up. Ask the investors in Facebook why they handed their money over to Mark Zuckerburg's dream. They did it because Facebook's trust factor is high among the majority of its members – the same people who disclose some of their most private moments and details online.

> *"Pretend that every single person you meet has a sign around his or her neck that says, 'Make me feel important.' Not only will you succeed in sales, you will succeed in life."*
>
> **Mary Kay Ash**

You're the Brand

American fashion designer, Tom Ford led Gucci from near bankruptcy in 1999 to a £2 billion brand before he left them in 2004. Ford was Gucci's main salesperson. His creative expertise brought the brand to life, and his character and charisma communicated its enormous value. Ford is doing the same thing today with his global fashion empire Tom Ford. A salesperson can learn two significant things from Ford – be intimately market aware and sell with style. Ford is the brand. Every salesperson is the brand too when they meet today's customer. That meeting can be face-to-face, by phone, or online in spoken and written words, or through the pictures they present.

You'll soon discover many WOW secrets of the leaders of many of the world's biggest brands, and I promise that their sales secrets will be workable, practical, and profitable for your company and you. I've carefully selected leading salespeople and a diverse supporting cast from the world of online and real world B2B (Business to Business) and B2C (Business to Consumer) sales. I've also selected some examples of WOW from the worlds of show business, sport, and politics. I don't know if you'll like them all, but I believe you'll like the wisdom they offer. They can help you satisfy today's customer's needs and wants more intimately.

The lead roles are held by Oprah Winfrey (Harpo), Phil Knight (Nike), Donald Trump (Trump International), Ray Kroc (McDonald's), Dermot Desmond (Celtic Football Club), Akio Morita (Sony), Bill Gates (Microsoft), Sam Walton (Wal-Mart), Indra Nooyi (PepsiCo), Steve Jobs (Apple), and Estée Lauder (Estée Lauder Companies, Inc). The supporting cast is powerful too. It includes leaders like Denise Morrison (Campbell Soup Company), Richard Branson (Virgin), Jeff Bezos (Amazon), Vittorio Colao (Vodafone), Martin Sorrell (WPP Group), Lawrence Tomlinson (LNT Group), Michelle Mone (Ultimo bra creator), Karren Brady (West Ham United), Sarah Blakely (Spanx), Howard Schultz (Starbucks), Marissa Meyer (Yahoo), and Rich Teerlink (ex Harley Davidson). These influencers developed a vision and sold it to their employees, sold it to their investors, sold it to their partners, and then they sold it to the rest of the world. They also proved that the biggest sales you'll ever make will always be to yourself. After all, if you don't believe in yourself, your products, and your services, no one else will.

PART 1.

1. Gratitude for Growth

2. Values for Victory

3. Energy for Excellence

4. Listening for Luck

5. Sharing for Success

6. Network for Net Worth

1. Gratitude for Growth

*"Gratitude is not only the greatest of virtues,
but the parent of all the others."*

Cicero

- ☐ The Gratitude Trilogy™
- ☐ Personal Gratitude - Bouncing Back
- ☐ Company Gratitude - Talk Your Way to the Top
- ☐ Basket Case to Brilliance
- ☐ Customer Gratitude - Selfish or Selfridge
- ☐ Today's Global Customer
- ☐ The Soldier, the President, and the Queen
- ☐ Today's Culture Club
- ☐ Today's Customer's Spirit

- ☐ **HELLO PROFIT Challenge I**

    Gratitude Generator – Personal
    Gratitude Generator – Company
    Gratitude Generator – Customer

The Gratitude Trilogy™

You can't sell with WOW unless you have gratitude. Gratitude is awakened appreciation for your gifts and possibilities. It empowers you and your company every day. You need what I call The Gratitude Trilogy™ - personal gratitude, company gratitude, and customer gratitude. Each one is a positive story that transforms possible complacency and negativity into personal and professional victory. If you stop, think, and look around your company, and towards today's customer, you can appreciate the resources that can make you a more successful salesperson. I'm constantly dumbfounded when I see and hear a salesperson make an excellent job of underselling their company. It's simply because they create excuses instead of championing their resources and opportunities.

When the rapper Curtis "50 Cent" Jackson was spotted drinking Vitamin Water, the product's owners asked him if he would promote it. You may think that's an example of gratitude for the rapper's profile, but the story gets better. "50 Cent" declined their suggestion, but he offered to become the company's creative partner. Think about his mind-set. He had gratitude and value for his abilities, his marketability, and the product's possibilities. When the company was sold to Coke for $4.1 billion, "50 Cent" earned $100 million.

Think about Ruth Handler. She was on holiday with her family in Switzerland when she spotted a comic-strip character doll in a shop window. It was called a *Lilli Doll*. She thought that she could make the doll more friendly and childlike. She also thought that she could name the doll after her daughter Barbara. Do you know that *Barbie* is the world's biggest selling toy ever, and it all started with Handler's awareness and gratitude?

When Henry Ford wanted to hire a senior leader, he took the candidate to lunch first. If the candidate put salt on their food before tasting it they never got the position. Ford believed that adding salt before tasting any food suggested an impatient, ignorant, and disrespectful mind-set. He knew he couldn't afford to have reckless decision makers on his team. That's the kind of mistake that can cost your company and your career dearly.

One of today's biggest business problems isn't a lack of resources and opportunities; it's a lack of resourcefulness and optimism. When you feel gratitude, you never dismiss the vitality of your career, or the needs and wants of today's customer.

Personal Gratitude - Bouncing Back

Gratitude becomes a powerful habit when you regularly reflect on and appreciate the gifts that life has bestowed and will bestow on you. These gifts can include your health, your family, your friendships, your company, or your career success. In 2012, I watched a programme called *High Flyers* on Bloomberg television, and I almost leapt from my sofa with excitement. The host Haslinda Amin interviewed one of the youngest men on Indonesia's Rich List. His name is Sandiaga Uno. He lost his job in finance in Singapore in 1997, but he recovered to co-found Saratoga Capital, and he's now worth over $700 million. We all love a comeback story, but it was a word he used that excited me most. When Uno lost his career, he was forced to return to his parents' home in Jakarta, Indonesia with his wife and children. He told Amin that he used to feel down, and he wanted to give up on his plans several times every day. However, one word gave him the strength to survive. That word was 'gratitude.' Uno's father showed him the concept of gratitude as enshrined in his faith. He reminded Uno that he should be grateful for his food, family, place to live, and his exceptional talents. It was further proof for my belief that gratitude is the foundation for every success. If you want a winning attitude, you must have a positive attitude; that starts with gratitude.

This is crucial because your attitude towards your career influences your career's attitude towards you. Your attitude towards today's customer also influences their attitude towards you. Gratitude protects you from the negative thoughts that can drain your mental and physical energy. It disables the forces of anger, disappointment, jealousy, and other vampires that can damage your emotional, intellectual, and physical capabilities to communicate. It's impossible to be a great salesperson – one who smashes targets and has fun doing it, without this foundation.

Company Gratitude - Talk Your Way to the Top

Business today is show business. When you put your company's promotional video online you better make sure it's got WOW. The competition for your video is every other video on YouTube that distracts today's customer from your message. Many companies spend a fortune to create a company video that receives only 82 hits. Most of those hits are from the people who made the video and the company's employees. A marketing expert told me that 'hits' stands for *How Idiots Track Success*. I don't want to sound harsh, but I care too much for you to waste your time and money creating a video that does you harm. I'm not saying that you need to book Steven Spielberg or James Cameron to direct your company video, but you must do it with WOW. With that in mind, let's look behind the success of one of the world's greatest ever salespeople. She's an expert in the show and the business of show business. You're about to discover some of her WOW secrets that will help you connect with today's customer. You might not sell what she does, but there's a lot you'll learn from her 28 plus years at the top of her game.

Oprah Winfrey was born on 29 January, 1954 in Mississippi. In that same year, a case called *Brown v Board of Education* went before the Supreme Court: the verdict allowed black people to have equal education rights. Perhaps Oprah's greatest talent is her ability to magnify small moments of fortune and use them to create bigger and better things. She's the woman who brought emotional intelligence to daytime TV and proved herself as one of the greatest communicators in the world. In 1986, *The Oprah Winfrey Show* was rated the most watched talk show in the history of TV. It's astonishing to think that Oprah's career was still in its embryonic stage back then. She was nominated for an Oscar; she created her magazine Oprah; she launched the careers of many people, and she supported the most worthy causes of all.

Oprah is a megastar company chairwoman and an everyday woman who appeals to all cultures, beliefs and every other diverse segment of society. That's not easy to achieve. Think about the brands she's created - Oprah, The Oprah Winfrey Show, HARPO, Oprah's Book Club, Oprah & Friends, and The Oprah Winfrey Leadership Academy for Girls. Her latest venture, OWN network reached success in two years when the industry average is five years.

When Oprah was discovered in Chicago in the 1980's, she was promoted by the late Roger King, a media executive of King World Productions and CBS Television. King is a Broadcasting & Cable Hall of Fame legend. His career includes the sale of syndicate rights for shows like *CSI*, *Everybody Loves Raymond*, and *Survivor*. He knew that selling Oprah wouldn't be an easy task. When she was starting out, King travelled around America to make sure Oprah got the break she deserved. One piece of strategic sales brilliance helped

1. Gratitude for Growth

launch Oprah. He convinced the secretaries of leading decision makers at TV companies that Oprah was a hugely appealing TV host. The secretaries told their leaders they preferred Oprah to the usual preachy white male host with perfectly combed hair. Oprah eventually became the ordinary billionaire whom women and men wanted to share their lives with. It's no surprise that Oprah is so honest and open about her respect and gratitude for King and other people who've helped her.

On Oprah's last show on cable TV, she spoke about her deep sense of gratitude for the "privilege" of doing her job. She called gratitude "the single greatest treasure" she gained from her work on the show. Oprah spoke about "opportunity" and "honour" and how her last show wasn't bittersweet. She said it was "all sweet, no bitter." Her audience was reminded of the gratitude journals and "the yellow brick road of sweet blessings." Is Oprah really a great salesperson? Yes, she is. Every day she sells her brand of self-help and hope through her TV show, magazine, and other marketing ventures. Her brand of self-love is a form of inner revolution. It's a brand that grows through the authentic conversations it creates. Oprah's selling succeeds because it's authentic: she communicates with gratitude and humility.

Her lesson of gratitude proves that no one is self-made. Isn't it true that your position in life is a result of inspiration offered from one or a variety of sources? Would Mozart have been as good if his father had not been a famous composer, a music teacher, and an author of a book on violin construction? What if his father had been a funeral director? Would Henry Ford and Thomas Edison have been as good as they were if they had not bounced brilliant ideas off each other? Would Elvis have dominated pop culture if he'd never heard the magnificent gospel singers in his local church? If you're gracious and appreciate the input of other people, you'll remain open for further strategic and personal support. Did Starbucks make the first cup of coffee or Nike make the first pair of trainers? No,; they showed gratitude for a commodity and they turned their versions into more desirable products. Then they sold them with WOW.

Oprah proves that company gratitude is necessary for success. In *Season 25: Oprah Behind the Scenes*, we got to see Oprah's gratitude for her team at HARPO. That gratitude was evident in good times and bad times, and it inspired devout enthusiasm from her team. It also helped create some of the most powerful and soul searching interviews ever seen on TV. Oprah knows that you can develop gratitude, but you can never fake it. If you try to fake it, the camera will tell the world because the camera never lies.

Basket Case to Brilliance

I hope the vision of one of Ireland's most respected and influential businessmen will inspire you to activate a deep sense of gratitude. Dermot Desmond is the owner of Celtic Football Club. It's one of the best run clubs in the world. It owns all its assets, is debt free, and it always makes a profit. Desmond is the chairman of IIU (International Investment & Underwriting). IIU specialises in direct equity investment and underwriting, funds management and capital markets trading. When Desmond was asked by the Irish Government in the eighties to help them create ideas to generate revenue, he put forward the idea for the International Financial Services Centre in Dublin. Desmond's vision was disregarded by many people in Dublin, but he understood two things. He believed in Ireland's intellectual capital, and he knew how to direct the country's competitiveness. Desmond sold his vision successfully despite the rebuffs by faceless government mandarins. They had bought into the belief that Ireland really was an economic basket case. However, Desmond had WOW ideas.

A derelict site in Dublin's Docklands is now home to more than half of the world's top 50 financial institutions including Citibank and

Commerzbank. Although the modest Desmond lays all the praise at the feet of his team and mentors, you should think about how the genius of his idea can help you. Let it inspire the creation of greater possibilities for the products and services you sell. Ireland was in deep trouble, but Desmond showed gratitude for what it had to offer and he sold that vision to the world. Desmond also activates gratitude in other areas. He's the chairman of *Respect*, a charity that supports people with mental and physical disabilities. A great salesperson today has Desmond's 'glass half-full' mind-set. It's the foundation of all innovation and success.

"Gratitude is the spark."

Darren Kelly

Customer Gratitude - Selfish or Selfridge

In 1909, an American called Harry Selfridge turned an undesired street into London's crowning thoroughfare - Oxford Street. He was ridiculed at the time, but he held a vision of creating a shopping experience with WOW. What was Selfridge's biggest talent? He noticed that many stores drove more customers away than they attracted. Why was this? Their owners believed that an ordinary customer was beneath them and lucky to be buying from them. Selfridge thought differently. He was grateful for every customer, and because of that sense of gratitude he was able to think deeply about their desires.

He believed a respectable customer should not be insulted just because thieves operated in stores. That's why he removed the stock from the store's protective shelves and placed them on counters for a customer to see and feel. He accepted that a customer may want to buy a gift, but they may find gift buying confusing. That's why he introduced the gift voucher. He knew that first impressions are paramount. That's why he put designers in charge of ground floor window displays. He knew that a fabulous window display attracts people like the rabbit hole in *Alice in Wonderland*. That's why his designers kept the window lights on at night, so the displays worked 24 hours a day to advertise the store.

Selfridge also accepted that everyone couldn't afford the Selfridges brand. However, he understood that they might be able to afford it one day. That's why he encouraged them to engage with the brand by creating a bargain basement for old stock. The shopping bags they carried around London advertised Selfridges. He knew that shopping was a pleasure, but not always a necessity. That's why he created the annual sales to appeal to a customer's curiosity and desire for an exclusive event. He also understood the power of events like Christmas. That's why he aligned them to his store. He reminded everyone about the number of shopping days until Christmas.

Gratitude is the foundation of creativity. You must look at what you have and get creative about ways to magnify its value for today's customer. Selfridge accentuated the positive because he recognised the fact that every customer wanted their shopping fantasy fulfilled. His gratitude allowed him to stand in their shoes. That's why he made them feel like stars. He patrolled the floors every morning to ensure every customer received red carpet treatment. He was meticulous about removing all dust from the counters and putting smiles on the faces of his employees. He also demanded that every employee possess deep knowledge of the store's products.

His critics may say he squandered his fortune, but his defenders will say he introduced quality when he proclaimed, "the customer is always right." He proved that selfish thoughts paralyse your ability to serve successfully. Many of the things we take for granted today are a result of his vision. If he was alive today, he would probably be creating the most elegant and effective shopping experiences online and offline.

Today's Global Customer

The world is witnessing a severe form of economic rebalancing, and that's exciting news or terrible news depending on your mind-set. In 2012, Jeff Immelt, the leader of General Electric spoke to Charlie Rose on CNN about how to succeed today. He said that you must be prepared to go to where the business is. That's why General Electric "sell all over the place." He also said every administration had to be "selling us" in a global economy. Did you notice the words "sell" and "selling"? Immelt highlighted the fact that we all need to sell, but he proved that selling requires action that many people don't want to take. The business is out there; it's just moved.

If you're willing to accept that and embrace the global market, you can succeed. You may have to leave Delhi for Dallas, Bangkok for Beijing, or Lahore for London. You can't lament the loss of local business and decide to sit it out and wait for it to return. If you do, you can face serious trouble. You must be grateful for globalisation, and you must be prepared to adapt to the differences that exist behind and beyond your own front door. In 1979, British company JCB, under Sir Anthony Bamford expanded into India. British technology company Dyson sells its products in over 50 countries. Even Harrods, Britain's largest upmarket department store delivers its goods to more than 40 worldwide destinations.

Denis O'Brien is Ireland's richest man. He was my boss when I worked as a radio personality on the Dublin station, 98FM. He's also the owner of Digicel, a mobile phone network provider that operates in 31 markets across the Caribbean, Central America, and Oceania regions. O'Brien was a panel member at the Ernst and Young, World

Entrepreneur of the Year Award event in Monaco in 2013. He spoke about Burma's promise when he revealed that only seven to eight per cent of the country's 63 million people had a mobile phone. He also spoke about how emerging markets are high growth markets.

O'Brien's consortium wasn't successful in its Burmese licence bid, but his philosophy reminded me of the mythical story of two shoe salespeople who went to visit a tribe in the Amazon jungle. One salesperson returned to his company and said there was no market because the tribe didn't wear shoes. The other salesperson returned to his company with excitement saying that the market was perfect. He revealed there was no competition, and the tribe unquestionably needed shoes to protect their blistered and battered feet. When you possess gratitude for globalisation you can explore areas for profit with empathy and real value.

If you own a website, you've got a global business. You may not choose to sell globally, but the option is there. When an economy suffers a downturn, you can survive by adapting to global demands. Starbucks teach a lesson in how you can sell in diverse markets. It's not about preaching to a market, but aligning with it before integrating with it. In 2012, Starbucks CEO, Howard Schultz appeared on *Talk Asia* on CNN to discuss his company's new coffee stores in India. His conversation proved once again that gratitude for globalisation is essential today. Schultz revealed that every coffee bean that Starbucks sold in India was grown and roasted in the country.

Schultz also revealed every detail in Starbucks stores fused respect for Indian culture and the Starbucks experience. The photographs on the wall highlighted Indian culture, but the small coffee cup image gave them "a wink of Starbucks." When he spoke about the food, he said it was created specifically for Indian tastes. Starbucks 'wink' offers the answer for connecting with new markets: have gratitude for the opportunity to embrace these new markets, and please do your homework. It's no coincidence that the salespeople who say they don't have time for reflection and appreciation will also tell you about how worried, negatively stressed and upset they are that business isn't as good as it should be.

Is Howard Schultz a great salesperson? He's a Xerox sales training programme graduate who also studied communications, and he trained in public speaking. He proves that selling with WOW creates profit. Schultz also teaches a lesson that you must be culturally aware in your own neighbourhood. There was a time when companies worried that communication was an issue when connecting with cultures in different parts of the world. These companies are sensitive to the fact that a multicultural society exists in the majority of communities they operate in.

Homogenisation is no longer appropriate across borders or within them. Success today depends on greater understanding, respect and appreciation of today's customer's culture. In other words, it requires gratitude. Your future success may only need a relocation of effort within the boundaries of your own country or city, but the same global principles apply. In 1998, Schultz allowed former basketball star Magic Johnson to open his first Starbucks franchise in Baldwin Hills, South Los Angeles. Starbucks integrated with the community, and as the coffee roasted, the sounds of Motown played to its predominantly black customers. The area had previously been a no go area for investors, but Schultz paid attention to Johnson's understanding of the local market, and the business grew rapidly. Starbucks know how to sell coffee with WOW. Their high quality coffee is matched by their in store smell and their meticulous customer service. They create an intimate, engaging, and safe third place to relax. You can't sell with that sort of WOW unless you possess gratitude that drives deep customer understanding.

The Soldier, the President, and the Queen

If you ask a leading general in any great army, they'll tell you that an understanding of different cultures is paramount today. The traditional soldier must be analytical and empathetic in their communications. How else can they build trust with different cultures? Yes, even soldiers are salespeople. They must have a curious mind and love learning about other people and their culture.

Does a president or a queen honestly have to act as a salesperson for their nation? Do they truly have to bother studying another country's culture? When Barack Obama visited Ireland in May 2011 to claim his Irish heritage, he connected with his audience by repeating his most famous words in Irish. In the centre of Dublin, "Yes We Can" turned into "Is Féidir Linn." Maybe Obama noted that Queen Elizabeth II won the Irish nation over that same month with a few Irish words too. The Queen opened her address at the state banquet by thanking her host, President Mary McAleese, in Irish. She said: "A hUachtaráin agus a chairde" – "President and friends." Such genuine respect and cultural understanding never fail to raise a smile. Was Obama selling himself with WOW to every Irish-American voter, and was the Queen selling a vision with WOW for Anglo-Irish relations? Yes, they were.

A great salesperson is always grateful for the opportunity to open their mind in today's global economy. They know that just because you can speak a foreign language doesn't mean you can communicate with today's customer. You must understand the deep motivations that influence today's customer's thoughts and behaviours. That foundation, built on gratitude helps you communicate with utter conviction. Every salesperson can learn from Obama and the Queen. A person's culture can represent a road map for their future. They may feel comfortable and part of a group that works in unison and obeys the same rules. If you do something entirely different to what they normally expect, it will take longer for you to build rapport. The world's most famous hotels welcome people from every part of the world. They know that they must be aligned to many cultures to offer them a homely environment for a memorable stay. This helps them create WOW moments. The opposite to WOW is OUCH. Isn't it wise to avoid the awkward situations that can arise when you offend another person, without even understanding why or how you did it?

> *"Cultivate the habit of being grateful for every good thing that comes to you, and to give thanks continuously And because all things have contributed to your advancement, you should include all things in your gratitude."*
>
> **Ralph Waldo Emerson**

Today's Culture Club

China and India, with a combined population of over 2.5 billion continually demonstrate their gratitude for the opportunities that a global economy offers. At the *Fortune Global Forum*, June 6-8, 2013, China's economic evolution under President Xi Jinping was discussed. The country has plans to transform itself from a predominantly manufacturing and exporting country to a services industry leader. India has already developed a positive global reputation for software development. So a salesperson's local market today will also be China and India's market tomorrow. That's a significant reason why today's salesperson must improve their game tenfold.

In his brilliant book *What Chinese Want*, Tom Doctoroff talks about the Chinese conflict that exists between communism and capitalism. He points to the fact that China's entrepreneurial, passionate, and cautious nature is still governed by its adherence to the rules of its 5,000 year civilisation and the ancient influence of Confucianism. As Martin Sorrell, the leader of WPP Group states in the book's foreword, "translation" is simply not enough today. Like Obama and Queen Elizabeth II demonstrated, translation only works when it's supported with deep respect and understanding. Sorrell enlightens every salesperson by saying that China is expanding way beyond its borders, so an understanding of Chinese culture isn't just a courteous thing to have. It's a crucial skill to help you sell inside China, and to sell to China's high spending elite who are investing on every continent. Sorrell reveals that many shops in London's Bond Street hire mandarin speakers and train them in Chinese etiquette so they can serve their rich Chinese shoppers more elegantly. This is a great example of selling with WOW. So forget about just doing the deal. You must develop gratitude for the culture you seek to influence. It's what a great salesperson does.

Let's take a look at some examples where cultural ignorance can affect a relationship with today's customer. In many parts of Chinese culture, it's wise to use both hands when offering a gift to a person. It's seen as hugely respectful. The oldest person is always greeted first, and many Chinese people will look towards the ground when greeting you. Face-to-face meetings, rather than written or phone conversations are the preferred business communication way for Chinese people. You must never do anything that makes a Chinese person lose face such as highlighting their errors or weaknesses. The key thing to remember is that their ambition is more subtle than the western world way. However, they are keen to adapt to other cultures. In 2013, The Sunday Times reported that one of the world's biggest train manufacturers, Chinese South Locomotive & Rolling Stock (CSR) teamed up with Northampton University in England. Chinese students have the opportunity to use their English language skills in an environment that will help them adopt the best British management skills. They include the communication skills to help the students adjust to British cultural and social issues. It's further proof that a salesperson today must appreciate and understand cultural differences.

Africa is a fast growing continent thanks to it having China as both a customer and an investor. Commodity prices also help, and Africa's technology sector is the fastest growing in the world. Nairobi in Kenya is known as the continent's Silicon Valley. Its banking system is underdeveloped, but its M-Pesa system (M is for mobile and Pesa is Swahili for money) according to *Time* magazine in 2012 exchanges 20% of its GDP using this SMS-based money transfer system. An insight into Kenyan culture can be gained by simply looking at its national flag. There are three horizontal stripes on the Kenyan flag. Black represents the Kenyan people. Red represents the blood lost during the fight for independence. Green represents agriculture. A thin white stripe divides each colour. The Masai tribe's shield and spears act as the protectors of all three. So while the country's mobile technology is positively changing the way investors look at Kenya, it still has its own culture and way of doing things.

Countries like Nigeria and South Africa also have elements you must understand. While selling in Nigeria, you must never use your left hand to give or receive. The left hand is considered unclean. In South Africa, Cape Town's dress code for sales meetings is less formal than Johannesburg. If a South African says 'just now' in reference to a time, it may not mean 'immediately', so you must determine the precise time.

When meeting people, have you ever thought you may be invading their personal space? A three feet distance is a North American's protection zone, while in Latin America, it's two feet. Retreating during a conversation is also considered incorrect in Latin America. If you're grateful for the diversity of this world, you'll be more willing to respect, understand and serve today's customer more effectively.

I'm not suggesting a study of world culture for you to improve your customer service. However, an effort to understand and respect another person's interpersonal guides will help you build and maintain rapport more easily.

It's worth listing seven new things you've learnt this year about the different culture of someone you work with or serve. Think about how this will improve your rapport and general conversations with them. This form of high customer awareness will give you an exceptional ability to empathise and serve. In many countries, including China and India, their brightest minds attend compulsory finishing schools to help them communicate the western world way. Don't you think you're halting your own progress if you don't show them the same respect?

> *"There is a great difference between knowing and understanding: you can know a lot about something and not really understand it."*
>
> ## Charles F. Kettering

Today's Customer's Spirit

Isn't it true that a person's spiritual upbringing can be their guide through life, and it can influence their personal and professional decisions? Isn't it a vital sign of respect for a person when you try to understand and respect their inner guide? A few years ago, a Muslim customer of mine said the following words during the fourth week of Ramadan. "I ask you every week if you want a drink, but you say 'no'. You say that because you know that I can't have one too." I thought it would be terribly unfair of me to drink a glass of water in front of him while he was thirsty. He took it as a major sign of respect and support.

I know that during Ramadan, the ninth month of the Islamic year, Muslims must fast, with no sex, no food, no drink, and no smoking allowed, from break of dawn until sunset. I apply the same respect for every other faith too.

Many companies apply the lessons learnt from leading religions in their marketing strategy. Spiritual beliefs teach us a lot about brand divergence. Al and Laura Ries point this out in their wonderful book *The Origin of Brands*. Islam, as they highlight is divided into Sunni and Shiite, and they also point out the divisions in Christianity, Judaism, Buddhism, Hinduism and other religions. You can only sell with WOW if you adapt to these divisions. Just ask McDonald's. They only introduced fish on the menu because some Catholics didn't eat meat on Fridays. It shows that it genuinely does pay to understand and respect a person's spiritual beliefs.

I'm not suggesting you sign up for a theology degree to improve your customer service, but a little study or enquiry can prevent you sounding ignorant at best. It's worth listing seven things about the faith of a customer you serve. In most cases, you'll open your mind to new ways to serve them more effectively. After all, it worked for McDonald's.

HELLO PROFIT Challenge 1

Gratitude Generator - Personal

Think about a person who helped you, whether they're a family member, a friend, a customer, or a stranger.

- ☐ What did they do to help you?

- ☐ When and where did this happen?

- ❐ What did they say?
- ❐ What did you say?
- ❐ What did you do?
- ❐ How did it improve your personal life?
- ❐ How did it improve your professional life?

Think about a customer you helped.

- ❐ When and where did this happen?
- ❐ What did you say?
- ❐ What did they say?
- ❐ What did they do?
- ❐ How did it improve their personal and professional life?
- ❐ How did it improve your personal and professional life?

Now that you hold a greater appreciation of gratitude, ask yourself the following question. Do I leave today's customer feeling ignored or confused, or do I show gratitude for their business?

Gratitude Generator - Company

Let's look at your career to see if you feel gratitude for what you do. I advised a company that never appreciated the value of the products and services it sold. They went from customer to customer as if it was a straightforward process of giving and taking. I did a little exercise with them to discover the effects of their hard work on the lives of today's customer and the community they operate in. One member on the team told me how he saved a company £89,000 in a tax bill. The money saved, paid for new equipment that created three new jobs. I asked the person if his exemplary work affected the families of the three new employees and the company's ability to grow. His response highlighted a considerable success from his work. Then I asked him what resources he used to facilitate his work. By the time he finished he offered greater appreciation for his company's support, and he discovered other resources that can help him in future challenges. When you adopt gratitude for your company and the team you work with, you open your mind to greater resources to fulfil your success. Simply put; when your mind is engulfed in a state of gratitude, it helps free you from the agents of fear, distrust, envy, anger, resentment, and worry that can hurt your career.

Think about the last outstanding sales success you enjoyed.

- Who helped you most?
- What did they do?
- How efficient were they?
- What did they save you in time, energy, and expertise?
- How did you show your appreciation?
- Did you praise them publicly?
- Did they share in your success?

When someone helps you, please reward them, so they feel inspired to help you again. Don't use the line, "It's their job anyway." People love to be praised and rewarded. It also sends out a message to other people who'll support you when you need them most. Please remember that it's not enough to feel gratitude. You must show your gratitude too.

Gratitude Generator – Customer

Pick two countries from the emerging business world. List their 20 biggest problems or future challenges. Match your company's products and services with those problems and challenges today and in the future. Seek expert advice from international trade organisations and your local Chamber of Commerce. The greatest piece of business might be closer than you think. You can try the same strategy with emerging or fading businesses. What can you offer that will help them grow or recover?

2. Values for Victory

*"The value of achievement
lies in the achieving."*

Albert Einstein

- ☐ Take a Bow
- ☐ Decisions of Destiny
- ☐ Believe it or Not
- ☐ Inspirational Values
- ☐ Run for Your Life
- ☐ Goddess of Victory
- ☐ Inspirational Values
- ☐ Just Do it (Right)

- ☐ **HELLO PROFIT Challenge 2**

    Values that Hurt Profit

Take a Bow

You can't sell with WOW unless you have a set of WOW values. Normal values are behaviours or principles that are important to you and your company. WOW values are the same, but they integrate today's customer and the rest of society too. Can you reveal your WOW values in 15 seconds? If you can, take a bow. If you say, 'No not now' then please keep reading.

Selling involves making many key decisions. Many of them are on the spot decisions that you must make responsibly. If you make a wrong decision, it can have a catastrophic ripple effect on a sale, a day, a week, or even your career. Your decisions may relate to risk, delegation, change, price, delivery, or one of many other things. You normally make decisions based on the information you have and your beliefs about that information. Your beliefs will serve you well if you know how to research, weigh facts, avoid bias, evaluate options, prioritise options, predict outcomes, analyse setbacks, solve problems, and understand the possible effect of every decision you make. Your beliefs will help develop your values that will guide most of your decisions. Values help you make easier, faster, and more profitable decisions. Let's take an example. If you believe that today's customer is precious to your business, you'll never lie to them. You may be tempted, but your values of honesty and respect would override your temptation.

Let's look at the WOW values of three leading salespeople. Amazon CEO, Jeff Bezos told *Business Week* in 1999 that Amazon was "a customer company." Everyone else thought it was a book, music, video, and auction company, but Bezos set the record straight. His WOW values mind-set means that every decision Amazon makes puts today's customer's experience at its heart. Bezos' values include 'usefulness, consistency, and speed'. Do you have the same WOW values? When the late Steve Jobs launched the iPod in 2001 he said, "In our own small way we're going to make the world a better place." Many companies talk about innovation, but their innovation is for their purposes only. Jobs eye for beautiful design and the integration of the customer experience made him a star. His WOW values included 'purity and simplicity' for today's customer. Do your WOW values appreciate today's customer as much as that?

Former fax machine salesperson, Sarah Blakely created the shapewear brand, Spanx to help women "look and feel their absolute best." Blakely's company grew out of her desire to hide her own cellulite and look and feel fabulous. Spanx's success has helped Blakely become the world's youngest self-made female billionaire. To her credit, her company has never veered away from those founding WOW values of 'empathy, beauty, and quality'. Blakely donated $1 million to Oprah Winfrey's Leadership Academy for girls in South Africa, and she became the first female billionaire to donate half her fortune to the Bill Gates and Warren Buffett *Giving Pledge*. Blakeley proves that her WOW values are real. That's why we believe her when she says she wants to "make the world a better place …..one woman at a time." Do your WOW values improve the world one customer at a time?

Decisions of Destiny

WOW values positively affect every decision you make. Two Hungarian teachers Klara and László Polgár challenged a once popular belief that females couldn't succeed in areas requiring spatial awareness. The Polgárs decided to home-school their daughters and to teach them how to play chess as part of their studies. While the so called experts laughed, the Polgárs sold themselves on their WOW values for themselves and the world – 'equality, mastery, and adventure'. All three daughters became top 10 chess players in the world. Their daughter Judit became a Grandmaster at 15. It proves that anyone can learn almost anything with the right influence, support, and dedication.

Denise Morrison is the president and CEO of Campbell Soup Company. Her sister is Maggie Wilderotter, the chairman and CEO of Frontier Communications. Their dad, Dennis Sullivan decided to share his business skills with his daughters when they were young, so they could be ready to succeed when business attitudes to women changed. He taught them the art and science of selling, profit-margin goals, and how to inspire and lead. Dennis Sullivan made his decision based on the WOW values that were true for him and his family and the world – 'leadership, love, and intelligence'.

Jay-Z, the husband of music superstar Beyoncé Knowles, is another example of a person who used the power of his WOW values. When record labels refused to give him a record deal in the nineties did he say, "I must be no good"? No; he didn't. He decided to stay true to his personal and global WOW values – 'ambition, originality, and contribution'. He sold his music CD's from the boot of his car. Jay-Z is now on the *Forbes List* of the world's most powerful celebrities. His album *Magna Carta Holy Grail* sold over 500,000 units in its first week of release in 2013. He would never have sold a single record in the first place if he didn't have any WOW values. Please don't listen to the prophets of doom and deceit; make your own decisions based on your own WOW values.

Believe it or Not

Why do some salespeople never develop WOW values? First: they never ask any questions at all; they simply accept what they're told or experience. Second: they ask terrible questions. Third: they ask good and specific questions, but they never analyse, accept, or use the relevant answers to change themselves for their promised success. When you keep an open but challenging mind, you can eliminate the unfavourable beliefs that hold you back: you can also build on the ones that help create WOW values.

Isn't it true that we have all discarded some beliefs that we once thought were true? New information came our way, or we paused to question the validity of a belief, and our lives changed in an instant. Some people once believed that cigarettes were a healthy product that helped them relax. They thought they were cool. Why did they think that? Wasn't it because fortunes were paid for advertisements to help them associate relaxation and sophistication with the product? Now of course, the world knows better. Beliefs are formed from conversations we have with ourselves about information we receive and events we experience.

You should take time to examine the validity of your beliefs, so you can see if they're accurate and if they serve you. This process will save you from accepting beliefs that may be harmful to your career and life. You must understand your personal motivations. When you do, you'll be better equipped to understand today's customer's motivations. That's the only way you can truly sell with WOW and have fun while doing it.

Pick a belief you have about something you dislike or fear.

☐   When did you form the belief?

- ☐ How did you form the belief? Was it an event or a conversation?

- ☐ If it was a conversation, was the source or sources of information credible?

- ☐ Do they speak from a position of intelligent authority, and do they possess experience and success in the area?

- ☐ Do you admire and respect the person(s) who delivered the information?

- ☐ Is the person(s) simply the town critic or cynic?

- ☐ Do you have any credible information that contradicts the belief?

- ☐ Why and how have they come to their conclusion, and what's their evidence to support it?

- ☐ Who else of a similar or greater standing agrees with them? You must be careful that you don't allow another person's weak or mistaken beliefs to undermine your beliefs, or to become your beliefs.

- ☐ Does the belief support your success or hinder you in any way?

- ☐ Would you reject the belief if credible information proves you're wrong?

- ☐ Are you willing to accept the belief may have once served a purpose that no longer exists?

*"Hide not your talents
they for use were made.
What's a sundial in the shade?"*

Benjamin Franklin

Inspirational Values

Would you like to discover what your WOW values are and how you can manage to hold these values consistently? Pick the ten personal values that you cherish the most and you believe today's customer cherishes too. They could include

- [ ] Adventure, Ambition
- [ ] Balance, Belonging
- [ ] Consistency, Contribution, Courage
- [ ] Discretion, Diversity, Determination
- [ ] Empathy, Enthusiasm
- [ ] Family, Freedom, Friendship
- [ ] Generosity, Growth
- [ ] Health, Humility, Happiness, Honesty
- [ ] Independence, Intelligence

2. Values for Victory

- [ ] Justice
- [ ] Leadership, Love
- [ ] Mastery, Merit
- [ ] Openness, Originality
- [ ] Perfection, Positivity
- [ ] Quality
- [ ] Reliability, Resourcefulness
- [ ] Speed, Strength, Support
- [ ] Teamwork, Trust
- [ ] Understanding, Usefulness
- [ ] Vision, Vitality

When you compile your list, please put them in the order of most importance for you and today's customer. When you submit your personal and professional values to front of mind awareness, you're less likely to be diverted from them. You'll find your life will be more fulfilling, and your success will have better direction. If your top three are honesty, mastery, and positivity you would never allow mastery to override honesty. That means you would never violate your values by lying to today's customer. You would rather apologise for an error or reveal other truths. WOW values define a relationship of recurring profit.

> "Don't let your special character and values, the secret that you know and no one else does; the truth - don't let that get swallowed up by the great chewing complacency."
>
> Aesop

Run for Your Life

Let's look at a salesperson who used his WOW values of 'respect' and 'admiration' for athletes to help him dominate the world of sportswear. Phil Knight was born on 24 February, 1938 in Portland, Oregon. His father was a lawyer, and he encouraged Knight to achieve academic success. Knight attended the University of Oregon, and he earned a journalism degree, but his main passion was athletics. He loved running, and he achieved a personal best, four-minute, ten-second mile under the guidance of Bill Bowerman, who later became his business partner. It was while studying years later at Stanford Graduate School of Business for his MBA that he awakened to the fact that the sports business was his calling. He was asked to invent a new business, describe its purpose, and create a marketing plan for it. His paper was called, 'Can Japanese Sports Shoes Do to German Sports Shoes What Japanese Cameras Did to German Cameras?' When Knight started running, the trainers that were available were made from tyre company rejects and offshoots. A runner's foot suffered bruising and bleeding after a short amount of miles. American trainers cost around $6, which was far cheaper than the more comfortable German trainers at around $30. Knight wanted to provide the best trainers for athletes across the world. His paper at Stanford gave him an extra layer on the foundation for his dream.

Knight toured the world after he completed university, and he arrived in Japan in November, 1962. He was impressed by a brand of trainer called Tiger. He met the owner of the manufacturer, and before he left his factory, Knight had secured the distribution rights he needed. Setting up a business takes longer than most expect, and Knight had to wait patietly for the samples to arrive. A year later, while he was working as an accountant to pay his bills, the Tiger samples arrived. Knight sent some trainers to his ex-coach Bill Bowerman in the hope that he would buy or promote them. Bowerman loved the trainers so much that he shook hands with Knight on a partnership to set up Blue Ribbon Sports. The company was the predecessor to Nike.

Goddess of Victory

Knight made his first sales of the new trainers from the back of his car at race meetings across Northwest America. By 1969, his selling success allowed him to resign from his accountancy job, and he was now able to work full-time for Blue Ribbon Sports. The company started to grow, and a new name was suggested to fit into the plans for the brand. Nike is named after the Greek winged goddess of victory. Nike, the daughter of the giant Pallas was known by the Romans as Victoria, a name meaning victory. Knight revealed it was his friend Jeff Johnson, who suggested the name Nike for the company that was born in 1971. Other marketing costs were also kept low when a girl called Carolyn Davidson designed the famous swoosh logo for a paltry $35.

Knight has always claimed he's not a natural salesperson, but I disagree. He has an incredible ability to understand people's aspirations and desires for heroes in their lives. That's how Nike has always managed to mix the best of popular culture with the best tools and champions of sport. In 1984, basketball legend, Michael Jordan endorsed Nike, but some journalists thought it was a colossal error. The five-year contract was reputed to be worth $1 million for every year, and this seemed to be a gamble during tough economic times. Other people disagreed with Nike's decision for a different reason. This was America before *The Cosby Show* became a success, and some critics felt that a black basketball player wouldn't appeal to Nike's larger market. After all, Michael Jackson had only recently become the first black artist to appear on MTV.

The video for Jackson's, *Billie Jean* was rejected by MTV at first. However, a week after it went to number one on the American Billboard Chart; MTV decided to play it. Jackson's music touched the world's soul. In many ways, Knight achieved greater success by touching the souls and soles of the people who bought his trainers. He certainly sold with WOW. To Knight, Nike represented the WOW values of 'passion, adventure, freedom, health, happiness, and success'. When he said, meeting sports athletes "is a thrill," he meant it. Roger Federer, Rory McIlroy, and Serena Williams are just some of his sporting heroes.

> *"Nourish your values.*
> *They're your truth.*
> *Be complacent,*
> *and your value suffers."*
>
> **Darren Kelly**

Just Do It (Right)

You, like Nike, are dealing with a community that speaks to each other face-to-face or online, and when your products and services are discussed, you better hope they served, excited, and rewarded them. Shared WOW values create loyalty. Isn't customer loyalty your goal? A loyal customer is cheaper to sell to, is less price conscious, and is more likely to speak about you in glowing terms to everyone they know. Think about a purchase you made that thrilled you. Isn't it true that when you spoke about it, you became a great salesperson for the company? Doesn't it make sense to align your deepest WOW values with today's customer's WOW values? Isn't this the route to create an emotional bond that will give you greater success?

No one is perfect, and there will be times when your WOW values are tested. Staying true to them might seem like the wrong thing to do. Let's look at an example where Knight's WOW values were tested. In 1987, Reebok sold more trainers than Nike. Nike's authentic and performance-enhancing footwear was usurped by a fresh fashion-conscious brand. The Jane Fonda aerobics fad had swept the world and Reebok's stylish trainers became the must have thing for women. Knight pointed out to journalists that Nike was more into sports than style. However, Nike gained back the top spot after it improved its designs and pulled off an example of advertising genius.

In 1988, Nike told us to "Just Do It." These words appealed to the values people held. They wanted to feel rebellious without being unlawful. They wanted to feel edgy without being weird. They wanted success with freedom. Nike tapped into those values. *Advertising Age* put "Just Do It" in the top four advertising campaigns of the 20th Century. "Just Do It" was inspired by the words of a convicted murderer called Gary Gilmore. His last words on 17 January, 1977, before a firing squad ended his life were, "Let's do it!" Nike proved that inspiration and hope can even come from the most horrendous incidents in life. The slogan "Just Do It" has inspired people to lose weight, get fit, and find a job: it's also inspired average salespeople to rise to the top.

Knight knew that products never sell themselves, no matter how delightful they are. However, he knew that integrated WOW values create something beyond a customer base: they create a community of fans. Knight never presses the panic button because the reason for Nike's success is grounded in his WOW values. In 2013, *FTSE Group* recognised Nike's corporate responsibility standards, and *Fast Company* magazine named Nike the No. 1 Most Innovative Company in its ranking of the top 50 innovators in the world. It's further proof that great values create WOW.

HELLO PROFIT Challenge 2

Values that Hurt Profit

Today's customer will not always be profitable. They may cause you heartache and distract you from your core focus and happiness. You must assess the true cost of your relationship. The relationship may offer monetary payment, but it may also cause losses of time and deliver negative stress through poor values. These losses are not readily seen, but they're costly.

Pick ten values that you dislike the most. The purpose of this exercise is to highlight the values of others that may cause you negative stress. It will help you adhere to your values and also give you a greater understanding of other people's values. They can include

- ☐ Arrogance, Anger
- ☐ Bullying
- ☐ Deceit, Disrespect
- ☐ Greed, Gossip
- ☐ Hatred

☐ Inconsistency, Indifference, Indecision

☐ Laziness, Loudness, Late payment

☐ Poor time keeping

☐ Rudeness

☐ Selfishness, Stagnation, Swearing

☐ Unreasonableness, Unreliability

It's worth asking if today's customer's values cost you more than you think. This process will save you from blindly accepting beliefs that may be harmful to your career and life. That's the only way you can truly win today and have fun while doing it.

3. Energy for Excellence

*"Zest is the secret of all beauty
There is no beauty
that is attractive without zest."*

Christian Dior

- ☐ Energy to Compete
- ☐ Energy to Excite
- ☐ Energy for Giving Back
- ☐ The Image of Energy
- ☐ Body Language Secrets
- ☐ When Hands Betray
- ☐ Control Your Energy
- ☐ Energy Rebooted
- ☐ Bra-llelujah
- ☐ Sleep Your Way to Success
- ☐ The Trump Express
- ☐ Breath of Success
- ☐ Sell with Silence

- ☐ **HELLO PROFIT Challenge 3**

  Energy Booster

Energy to Compete

You can't sell with WOW unless you've got energy. Energy is the power that fuels your mental and physical activities. It affects how you think and feel, and it also affects how people think and feel about you. Have you ever noticed that the most successful people in sales have the type of energy that lifts themselves and the people around them? In 2013, before Angela Ahrendts announced she was leaving her CEO role at Burberry for Apple, she gave an incredible TED talk. She highlighted the power and force of personal energy for every human interaction. Ahrendts transformed Burberry after she became its CEO in 2006. It has over $3 billion in sales, over 16 million Facebook fans, and over 2 million Twitter followers. Her TED (Technology Education Design) talk showed how emotive energy goes way beyond what's considered to be normal communication.

It's also true that physical energy can transcend normal communication. That's why a great salesperson treats their body like an athlete would. They know they need to be sharp and alert, and possess the emotional, intellectual, and physical stamina to sell with WOW. It's true that you'll meet the odd salesperson who does well while enjoying a long liquid lunch, or by overeating the wrong foods, but how do they feel inside? Are they truly enjoying their job if they've to drag their body around? Are they honestly alert and focused if they're slightly hazy from poor consumption? Are they equipped to respond quickly and effectively to the challenges of selling every day? When you look after yourself, you've got more energy to think clearly and solve problems more creatively. You'll also have high-energy to tap into your memory and recall what you need. Moreover, high-energy helps you enjoy better connections with people. It helps you to inform and influence more powerfully, and persuade more effectively. A great salesperson who enjoys a glass of wine or a beer restricts their drinking to times that never affect their professionalism. They love to have fun, but they make sure their fun never hurts their success.

Energy to Excite

Let's look at a salesperson and a leader who's regarded as a whirlwind in business. He's a man, who has the energy to get things done and sell with WOW. Donald Trump was born on 14 June, 1946 in Queens, New York. He's one of America's most famous businessmen, thanks to his flamboyant personality and straight-speaking media appearances. He's the Chairman and CEO of The Trump Organisation, a real-estate development company, based in New York. Trump was named "Visionary of the Century" by the UJA Federation. He can frequently be seen and heard saying, "You're fired," on the original *The Apprentice* TV show.

Trump has caused controversy in Scotland over his venture *The Great Dunes of Scotland* on the Aberdeenshire coastline. Can you imagine the controversy if he'd called them *The Donald Dunes?* Trump International Golf Links in Aberdeen has been placed in the top three golf courses in the world by Sandy Jones, the chief executive of the PGA. We should not be surprised. If you study reviews of Trump hotels by worldwide leisure critics, you'll see the same words coming up all the time – 'luxury, fabulous, one-of-a-kind, great design, glamorous, 5 star, opulent, and beauty'. Bear in mind that Trump is involved in every stage – planning, acquisition, finance, development, and the customer experience. You can't reach that level of success without incredible energy to support astute business acumen.

3. Energy for Excellence

His father Fred was a wealthy real-estate developer in Brooklyn, and a young Trump spent much time learning his negotiation skills with his father on various building sites. His business acumen is supported by a degree from The Wharton School of the University of Pennsylvania. Trump Tower in New York City stands as a majestic beacon for the brand, but perhaps the brand's greatest symbol is the one Trump created personally, when he came back from near bankruptcy in the 1990's. An average salesperson would have given up, but Trump didn't know how or when he should quit. His comeback has served as an inspiration for many other people who've rebuilt their careers.

He may be in the real-estate business, but he doesn't sell buildings. He creates and sells excellence and elegance with an energy that many can't match. When you see Trump, you see an impeccably groomed person who radiates self-assurance. He builds excitement, and his energetic confidence inspires others to take action. Trump is a business version of the former Aberdeen and Manchester United manager, Sir Alex Ferguson. Like Ferguson, he has the hunger to win every time. Like Ferguson, Trump knows how to get people's attention. After all, if you don't get people's attention, your message and your value are of no use.

Trump uses his high-energy to get more out of 24 hours than most. He doesn't drink or smoke, and he feels that this alone gives him a head start. Perhaps, his time spent in the New York Military Academy helped him develop a discipline that his competitors lack. He claims he advised his children, Ivanka, Eric, and Donald Jnr, not to drink alcohol, smoke, or do drugs. This is partly influenced by the fact that his older brother, Fred Jnr. died an alcoholic. It was Fred Jnr. who told Trump he should never drink alcohol. The other reason is that Trump has seen many business people degrade themselves when they're drunk. He finds it hard to respect people who lose control to that extent. When the Trump family appeared on The Oprah Winfrey Show, he referred to life as "fragile." He knows how lucky we are to be alive today, so he lives his life to the max with as much energy as he can use.

Energy for Giving Back

High-energy is also essential to help you achieve the true art of fulfillment. When you possess it, you can contribute more to your team, today's customer, and your community. Trump looked at the Wollman Skating Rink in Central Park, New York in 1986, and he decided that bureaucracy could no longer be allowed to prevent New Yorkers' enjoyment of a city treasure. Six years had passed since renovation work began, and New Yorkers were still without a place to skate in the park. Trump got involved and gave people a substantial reason to smile when he opened the rink on budget and within a time some people said was impossible to achieve. It was his energetic attitude that inspired a community to follow his vision. In short; he sold his vision with WOW.

> *"I speak two languages. Body and English."*
>
> **Mae West**

The Image of Energy

It was Freud who said, "No man can lie; he chatters with his fingertips." Body language tells another person how you think and how you feel. Think about Usain Bolt's body language before he won the 100m in the London Olympics in 2012. He looked relaxed as he pretended to play some songs as a nightclub DJ just before the start of the race.

After he won the race, he raised his hands in the air and smiled. We didn't hear Bolt say he was relaxed before the race or happy after it through his words. We knew that through his body language.

Trump understands the energy of interpersonal communication. You're judged initially by how you look, and secondly by what you say. So if you get the first wrong, your words will lose a large percentage of their power. A shabby look suggests to today's customer that you're disorganised, lazy, have poor self-esteem, or worse, you've got no respect for them. It also suggests that you're lacking in energy. If you lack energy, your body language will betray your words. It will feel like you're driving your sales career with the handbrake on.

Do you betray your expertise and integrity when you walk, sit, and embrace today's customer? Do you slouch when you face them and portray a careless attitude? Do you look everywhere but in their eyes when you're trying to influence and persuade them? Perhaps you do care, and I hope you do, but do you possess enough energy to combat Monday morning blues or Friday afternoon mediocrity? If you lack energy, you'll send the wrong messages to today's customer. Make no mistake about it. If your energy is low, it will affect your thoughts: your body language will reveal those thoughts. Tonya Reiman, the author of the brilliant book *The Yes Factor* is a great body language expert. She's a regular contributor on *The O'Reilly Factor* on Fox News. Her analysis of the body language of leading figures is both funny and frightening. She also proves that a conversation with today's customer can be a waste of time if you don't tune in to their body language.

You really don't have to be Dr. Cal Lightman (Tim Roth) from the hit TV series *Lie to Me*: just pay attention to see if today's customer is genuinely considering your offer of value. When they put a finger in their mouth, or place a palm on their cheeks they may be bored. When they scratch their chins they may be thinking about your words carefully. When they swallow, and increase their blinking rate, they may be lying to you. You need high-energy to be alert, so you can identify a real objection, or accept that you won't win that business. This will save you a lot of heartache if you can remain aware of what today's customer's body language tells you. *The Definitive Book of Body Language* by Allan and Barbara Pease is the best book on the subject in my opinion. They're certainly a couple who deliver their expertise with WOW.

Body Language Secrets

Let's take a brief look at Trump, and his apprentices' body language to discover their inner thoughts. You'll also discover similar body language in Lord Alan Sugar and his apprentices on the British version of the show.

When Trump is optimistic and energetic

- ☐ he rarely folds his arms.
- ☐ he leans toward his apprentices.
- ☐ he offers a warm and pleasant smile.
- ☐ his palms are open.
- ☐ his eye contact is relaxed.
- ☐ his jacket or coat is unbuttoned.

When Trump gets upset

☐   his brow is furrowed.

☐   his eyebrows face downwards.

☐   he stares.

☐   his voice gets louder and deeper.

☐   he points forcefully with his index finger.

When The Apprentice stars get nervous

☐   they giggle.

☐   their hands cover their mouths when they speak.

☐   they continually clear their throat.

☐   their faces reveal they're in a state of alert.

☐   they never sit on the whole chair.

☐   their head nodding speeds up.

When The Apprentice stars get frustrated

☐   they mess with their hair and jewellery.

☐   they take short breaths.

- ❏ they tap their fingers on the table.

- ❏ they look in different directions.

- ❏ they sigh or grunt.

When you're excited to deal with today's customer, you can't hide your feelings. Your pupils dilate up to four times their natural size and today's customer feels this subconsciously. Allan Pease once pointed out that many bestselling children's toys have enlarged pupils. Why? Children are attracted to larger pupils because they express excitement and happiness. This is because the eyes truly are the windows to soul of every human being. Warm eye contact is important because it reveals your sincerity and commitment. High-energy is essential to communicate such sincerity and commitment.

> "He, who has health, has hope;
> and he who has hope,
> has everything."
>
> **Thomas Carlyle**

When Hands Betray

Lack of energy can create errors in your body language that can hurt your communication. Have you ever noticed that you tend to fold your arms when you're tired or bored? You may also fold them out of habit, but this folding tightens your body and reduces your agility. Although folded arms only represent one word in a body language sentence, they send a message to today's customer that you're defensive, uninterested, or unwilling to be honest with them. So before you fold your arms out of habit again, think about Usain Bolt's race celebrations, and ask yourself the following question. Have I ever been truly excited in my life when my arms were folded? Before you answer that question, remember that body language is more honest and revealing than the words you use.

Your hands have 27 bones each and when they move they say a lot about you and what you're thinking. When your palm is open you display honesty and openness. When you place your palm down you suggest you're making an order. When you place your hands behind your back, you suggest you're hiding something. Remember that your hands are tremendously powerful in all your communication. They say something about you no matter where you put them. When Oprah Winfrey interviewed former Alaska Governor Sarah Palin and her daughter Bristol in 2010, the Palins didn't move their hands. Their clenched hands suggested that they were protecting themselves from saying something they may have regretted later on.

The energy of your handshake will also help you connect with today's customer. You don't want to shake their hand as if you're attempting a karate chop. However, you want enough energy to engage with an equally respectful handshake. A weak handshake can be explained by an illness that affects your hand, but not everyone thinks about such reasons. Today's customer simply accepts how they feel at any moment, and they may make unfair decisions about you.

Control Your Energy

Powerful gestures release negative or excess energy, and they support the power of your words. You'll notice that a great salesperson will naturally adopt the following gestures the most. That's because their words are powered by their energy and genuine passion.

1. Offer and Receive

Lay your hands out with your palms facing the sky. This gesture is highly effective when you're appealing to someone.

2. Togetherness

Place both your palms facing each other as if you're holding a football. This can be used when you suggest a coming together of people or ideas, or to reinforce unity.

3. Division

Turn your left or right hand into a knife with your palm facing inwards. Cut through the centre of the space in front of you to indicate division or separation.

4. Making a point

If you want to point, it's less aggressive if you hold a pen and use that to point for you. If you don't have a prop, I suggest you wrap your fingers around your thumb when you point. This stops you pointing with your forefinger, which can make you look aggressive.

5. Resting your hands

It's wise to have a resting place for your hands when you're not making a point. If you put your hands in your pockets and later try to make a hand gesture, your movement can create more swing than a Mike Tyson punch. A suitable resting place is just in front of your tummy. When you move your hands from that point, your action looks more graceful. Please also avoid playing with your hair, jingling coins in your pockets, playing with objects like pens or glasses, rocking to and fro, and twiddling your thumbs.

Energy Rebooted

Genetics, society's rules, and events in your day conspire against you having an energetic body, so you must actively decide to live with WOW. Do you eat nutritional foods and reduce negative stress? Do you exercise and rest effectively? I advise you to see a doctor before you undergo any changes to improve your lifestyle. All your achievements will mean nothing if you don't look after your health and fitness. You'll notice that I said health and fitness. An average salesperson violates their health by confusing health with fitness. They get drunk on Friday night and believe a 30-mile cycle the next day will undo the calorific effect of ten pints of beer. You don't have to be a medical expert to realise that this form of self-preservation is, in fact, self-harm.

A great salesperson knows that if you combine a poor diet, with punishing exercise or no exercise and a negatively stressed lifestyle, the only time you'll have time to switch off will be when you're ill. When I speak to any great salesperson, they tell me how they avoid the sugar roller coaster that picks you up in seconds, but quickly drops you for hours. Doctors tell us that sugar is also responsible for obesity, high blood pressure, mood swings, diabetes, tooth decay, and heart disease. Sugar has many names, such as mannitol, sorbitol, sucrose, glucose, fructose, and lactose. It pays to read your food labels. Ask your doctor or an expert nutritionist for their advice. *The 150 Most Effective Ways to Boost Your Energy by* Jonny Bowden is in my opinion the clearest, most informative, and entertaining book on the subject. Jonny is simply a passionate person who knows his stuff and he cares deeply about people.

Bra-llelujah

A woman who understands the importance of high-energy is bra tycoon, Michelle Mone, OBE. Her genius for comfort and style has women worldwide singing hallelujah. I enjoyed sharing the stage with Mone as she inspired an excited audience at the Buy Yorkshire Conference (England) 2013. Her company MJM International was the first ever UK lingerie company to show at New York Fashion Week. While growing up in Glasgow penniless her family suffered two tragedies. Her brother died aged eight and her father suffered from cancer and later paralysis. The inventor of the Ultimo bra left school at 15 with no qualifications.

However, Mone's intelligence, determination, and energy helped her succeed in the world of sales before she created a business that people like Rachel Hunter and Mel B have promoted. Her Hollywood moment came when her bra appeared in the movie *Erin Brockovich* as a support for Julia Roberts' cleavage. Ultimo became the choice of bra for an Oscar winner and the world. Mone's passionate desire to inspire people in business was noted, and it led to her role on the British TV show *The Apprentice: You're Fired!* Even Prime Minister David Cameron invited her to address the British Government. She understands the importance of high-energy to help her fulfil her goals.

Mone speaks honestly about how she felt when she was overweight, and how the healthy lifestyle she adopted gave her a new confidence. She was even persuaded to model her own products. Like every great salesperson, she knows that you can't operate every day without the right fuel and energy to fulfil your dreams. Many people have transformed their lives after hearing her story. Mone sells her story and her company's story in a way that mesmerises and inspires: it proves that the truth always wins. No matter where you come from, or what money you don't have, you can still become a success in whatever profession you choose. But you're going to need a lot of energy.

Sleep Your Way to Success

Good sleep is essential for your energy level. Some salespeople can thrive on four hours sleep, but many can't. I know one great salesperson who lives by the mantra, 'don't overcharge your sleep credit card'. He believes the interest is extortionate. However, the quality of your sleep is as important as the quantity. A friend of mine once asked how many hours sleep a salesperson needs. "That depends on whether you're worried, excited, overstimulated, ill, or disturbed by something else," I replied. You can get eight hours of restless sleep or five hours of peaceful sleep. Which one recharges you the most? There are sleep guidelines, but like everything else, sleep is personal.

"Discipline suffers when you run low on energy."

Darren Kelly

The Trump Express

Do you remember how you felt when someone said they truly respected you? You could tell they did, more from the way they said it than what they said. Their voice had natural richness of tone, volume, pitch, and pace that created a WOW moment. Does your voice suggest that you're excited about what you offer? When you say hello to today's customer, does it mean "I'm thrilled to see you," or does it suggest "I wish I didn't have to see you."

When you hear Donald Trump speak, you can understand why many people are drawn to his powerful voice. He has an amazing ability to hold his audience's attention with his articulate and energetic mix of Wharton scholarship, business acumen, and popular culture. Is it any wonder that the media take their cameras and microphones to Trump Tower to hear Trump's opinions? He can speak about China, OPEC, Obamacare, and Miley Cyrus in the same conversation, and somehow tie them all back to a special feeling about the Trump brand. The media know that Trump expresses a unique intellect and energy that captivates TV audiences. That's always great for ratings. Is it also any wonder that Trump is the highest paid public speaker in the world?

The American Spectator awarded Trump the *T. Boone Pickens Award* for entrepreneurial excellence and business leadership in 2013. It called him an "iconic entrepreneur" who "exemplified sustained success and management within the business world." His acceptance speech energised and inspired his audience. Trump accepted the realities of a world where "every penny counts," but he also said, "you can't have a death wish, and you have to be smart." He expressed his passionate views on how America could remain an economic super power and progress as it should. It proved that Trump may sell the Trump brand with WOW, but his patriotic desire to sell America's brand with WOW is just as impressive.

Breath of Success

A bad habit that reduces energy is incorrect breathing: it deprives you of the oxygen to nourish your brain and other vital organs. I recommend daily exercise and a deep breathing routine (in fresh and clean air) for three reasons.

- ☐ It improves your ability to concentrate and create.

- ☐ It helps reduce your stress.

- ☐ It helps you communicate with authority and clarity.

3. Energy for Excellence

The World Chess Championship 1972 is known as the Match of the Century. America's Bobby Fischer beat the defending champion, the Soviet Union's Boris Spassky. Before the match, Fischer began swimming underwater to build up his lung capacity. The reason seemed crazy to many people at first. Fischer had noticed that Spassky only ever lost games between the ninth and tenth hours of a chess match. When he lost, he looked burnt out. His shoulders drooped, his head dropped, and his back arched. Fischer believed that if he built up his lung capacity through exercise, he could process oxygen more effectively: this would power his brain in the heat of battle. Fischer became a champion because he recognised that the mind and body can't be separated.

A deep breathing routine is also important to reduce stress. An average salesperson spends too much time behind their desk. This results in shallow breathing habits; they breathe from the chest up. When I worked as a radio personality I was told to expand my tummy instead of my chest to inhale more oxygen. The air you inhale doesn't go to your tummy, but it forces your diaphragm down, and allows your chest to expand. Every intake of breath should be long and slow. This allows you to inhale a large amount of oxygen while relaxing you at the same time. This action actually soothes the organs in your tummy and sends more oxygen to feed your blood. The same speed should be used when you're exhaling.

When you have greater lung capacity you also enjoy greater control over your natural vocal delivery. You need enough air to deliver every sentence clearly. A salesperson with poor lung capacity skips words, shortens words, and loses clarity at the end of their sentences. Your head, shoulders, vocal cords, lungs, and diaphragm should work in harmony to help you project your voice effectively. The best time to take a deep breath during a conversation with today's customer is when they're speaking. The best time to take a deep breath during a speech or presentation is during your audience's laughter or applause, or during any interruptions.

Sell with Silence

When you hear a great salesperson communicate you'll notice their ability to pause. They're always in complete control of themselves and their message. They know that when they pause they allow today's customer to catch up. A pause also allows them to highlight something extremely valuable that's coming next. It can create anticipation, suspense, and excitement for today's customer. It also gives increased energy to their words.

When Amazon CEO, Jeff Bezos launched the Kindle Fire he held it in the air and paused to let his audience appreciate the device. When Pope Francis 1 appeared on the Vatican central balcony for the first time, people wondered if he would ever speak. His powerful pause helped create a WOW moment of happiness and reverence when he finally spoke. Is the Pope a great salesperson? Yes he is. In 2013, *Time* magazine named him *Person of the Year* because he gave the Vatican a victory by connecting with people with his energy and empathy. His powerful pause reminded me of a quote by Oliver Wendell Holmes. He said, "Talking is like playing on the harp; there is as much in laying the hands on the strings to stop their vibration as in twanging them to bring out their music." It's worth pausing right now to think about that.

Barack Obama is a master at using the power of a pause. There's a joke that says if you take a 15-minute Obama speech and cut out the pauses, the speech would only be two minutes long. A confident communicator, like Obama, never confuses energy with speed and never underestimates the power of giving an audience space. The pause is one of Obama's most valuable speaking tools. It empowers his audience to understand him, and it makes him look and sound in control.

HELLO PROFIT Challenge 3

Energy Booster

Complete this challenge to help boost your energy level. Please ask yourself the following questions for a brief energy check.

- ☐ Do I enjoy getting out of bed every morning?
- ☐ Does my energy level dip and climb throughout the day?
- ☐ Has tiredness recently helped create a mistake in my work?
- ☐ Do I wish I could remember things more easily?
- ☐ Am I able to work late without feeling tired?
- ☐ Does the slightest mistake, interruption, or setback stress me out?
- ☐ Do I catch colds easily?
- ☐ Do I find it hard to make decisions?
- ☐ Do I sleep well?
- ☐ Do I concentrate effectively?
- ☐ Do I relax without a myriad of worries on my mind?
- ☐ Do I recharge myself to avoid burnout?

☐ Does switching off and recharging mean doing something that's still work related?

☐ Do I help create an energetic environment for my colleagues, and today's customer?

If you answered any of these questions unfavourably you may wish to see your doctor. After all, energy is the power of life and fuel for your success. A great salesperson works with the same intensity and enjoyment on Friday at 4pm as they do on Monday at 10am. They couldn't do that if they didn't possess the energy to stay motivated, and the fuel to take incredible action.

4. Listening for Luck

*"Listening is an attitude of the heart,
a genuine desire to be with another,
which both attracts and heals."*

J. Isham

- ☐ Silent Listening
- ☐ Listen to the Whole Conversation
- ☐ Listen for Limitations
- ☐ Listen without Ego
- ☐ Listen Truthfully
- ☐ Responsive Listening
- ☐ WOW Listening
- ☐ The Listening Company

- ☐ **HELLO PROFIT Challenge 4**

  A Plan with Ears

Silent Listening

You can't sell with WOW unless you learn to listen. Listening implies that you concentrate on a sound or sounds, but an average salesperson never concentrates: there are two main reasons. We live in an information heavy world. When we suffer from information overload we stop listening. We also have many devices to record information. If we miss a message we know that it will probably be repeated again in an email, on a podcast, on a blog, or on a TV replay. The problem is that we may never get the time to check the recorded messages because every day brings more communication.

The exciting news is that if you become a great listener, you'll maximise your success as a salesperson. While everyone else fails to engage by listening effectively, you'll be the one who understands every subtle and obvious message. When you look silently into today's customer's eyes, they'll feel refreshed because they know you care. Listening attentively without any motive is a sincere form of respect. You're silently saying, "I'm interested in what you're saying." Did you notice that L-I-S-T-E-N is made up of the same letters that are in S-I-L-E-N-T? I wish I could claim that observation, but it comes from an unknown author.

Have you ever spoken to someone and their eyes revealed that they couldn't wait to push in and express their opinion, or speak about themselves? Did you notice their head nodding quickly and their eyes urging you to finish? Did you speed up your thought process and delivery only to be cut off in a mid-sentence? How did that make you feel? Did you feel there was no real communication? Did you feel that it was just an exchange of words?

Now think about this? Do you act like that when you communicate with today's customer? Are you so excited by what you offer that you can't control your urge to tell them all you know? This is what today's customer thinks when you don't listen. "He might as well have told me all he knew in an email or a brochure. I didn't feel a connection with him, and I'd find it hard to do business." Your desire to establish your expertise and offer value must never destroy your listening skills if you want to develop a relationship of trust and respect. An average salesperson enters a relationship with their sole focus being on their selfish agenda. This forces them to miss valuable information that today's customer offers. This isn't the way to sell with WOW.

Listen to the Whole Conversation

You weren't born a great listener, but you can become a great listener. Let's test your listening skills with a piece of music you love. Take your favourite song and try to figure out what instruments, languages, voices, and music styles are involved. If you pay attention to what you hear, you'll appreciate the importance of real listening. I love music, and listening closely to the expertise behind a song has helped me immensely. I've interviewed several leading singers and bands like George Michael, Cher, Lionel Richie, Duran Duran, and UB40. They told me how creating a song is like putting the pieces of a jigsaw together. There are many things such as chord progression, arrangement, strings, and phrasing. It's natural for you not to appreciate the depth of genius in a hit song, but you can't dismiss anything in a customer conversation.

You must remember to listen to all the pieces of a conversation if you wish to serve today's customer well. It's also worth spending a few minutes every day simply listening to your own thoughts. An average salesperson won't take the time to do this, but it worked for some of the greatest minds. Martin Luther King, Gandhi, and Nelson Mandela were forced to listen to themselves in enforced confinement, but you can do it within the freedom of your daily life. It will help give you greater clarity. The message here is that every conversation consists of a myriad of thoughts. You must remain awake to both the overt and underlying messages. You can't do that if you listen superficially.

> "Courage is what it takes to stand up and speak; courage is also what it takes to sit down and listen."
>
> **Winston Churchill**

Listen for Limitations

One person who understood the importance and art of intentional, intense, and empathic listening was a man who changed the way we eat. Ray Kroc was born on 5 October, 1902 in Oak Park, Chicago. He was a salesperson who bought a small hamburger business called McDonald's, and transformed it into the world's most successful fast food enterprise. Kroc, who made over $500 million in his career, was featured by *Time* magazine as an important and influential business leader of the 20th Century. Even if Kroc had sold computers or legal advice there's no doubt that McDonalds would outsell most companies today. Products, as Kroc knew aren't the ultimate differentiator. The ability to serve a desired experience with WOW is.

This isn't a story to support fast food, but a story to show you how a man, who never cooked a burger to sell, entered the industry in his fifties, and dominated it. It's also a story about how he developed a vision to build a business, and how he guided it sensitively until his desired results became real. It will show how listening acts as your compass for success because it forces you to accept your limitations. This allows you to correct any errors and improve on any decisions you make.

Kroc learnt the discipline and focus necessary for planning and listening success during the First World War. He trained to become an ambulance driver, but he missed the action because the war ended before he could be called to service. After the war, he worked as a paper-cup salesperson, and he enjoyed stints as a jazz musician and a salesperson at a radio station. He also tried to sell real-estate in Florida, but that didn't work out as expected. Kroc remembered returning to his home in Chicago after the failure. He said he was cold, hungry, and broke.

Kroc's life changed when he took a job as a Multi-Mixer milkshake machine salesperson with a brief to sell all across America. He noticed that, in California, the McDonald brothers, Dick and Maurice had purchased ten Multi-Mixers, so he decided to look deeper into their restaurant success. The Multi-Mixer machine he sold could make five milkshakes at a time. Kroc studied the McDonald's restaurant, and he was amazed at what he saw. Kroc listened carefully as the brothers explained how they had simplified their menu to nine items. Their *Speedee Service* system could sell more food to every customer. Kroc's mind raced with the possibilities of how powerful the brand could become under a franchise agreement, and he thought about how many Multi-Mixers he could sell to every franchisee.

Kroc befriended the brothers, and in 1954, they allowed him to sell franchises of their restaurant, but after years of hard work, he was barely making any money. In 1961, he purchased the company from the brothers. The agreement was for the McDonalds to receive $2.7

million, which gave each brother $1 million after taxes. Kroc admitted that he could've taken the knowledge he learnt from the brothers and set up the same operation under a different name for $2.7 million less, but he loved the name McDonald's. He knew the name would be a winner because it was warm and wholesome, and it would be accepted worldwide.

Kroc's most remarkable trait was his ability to listen to others, so they could help him develop a flexible plan to succeed. He possessed a vision for short-term and long-term success, and he used his resources to compete successfully in any market he chose. He made excellent decisions about choice of products, meeting the needs of every customer, gaining advantage over competitors, and exploiting and creating new opportunities. Kroc knew that when you plan, you develop focus, and when you're organised, you've room to be more creative. Creativity without organisation leads to a mess. However, like any great salesperson, Kroc knew that great plans must change when opportunities emerge. As my mentor Brian Tracy points out in his brilliant book *Flight Plan,* "Success is goals; all else is commentary." However, even if you create extensive plans, you'll always be off course for most of your journey. Your ability to make what Tracy calls "continual course corrections" requires incredible listening skills.

An average salesperson creates a plan and sticks to it rigidly. Even when things go wrong, they blindly stick to their plan, or even openly complain about it while they fail. Why does this happen? The truth is that an average salesperson hates to admit they've made a mistake. They find it more comfortable to run a strategy that's wrong than put their hands up and say, "Oops, let's rethink this." It sounds like a crazy concept, but it's happening all over the world. The key to flexible planning is to choose your dream, gather the facts, establish the plan, and to listen out for opportunities that can help you create your success more quickly, more easily, and more profitably.

Listening helps a salesperson understand the needs and wants of today's customer. It also keeps them close to where the next success could come from. When Kroc's associate, Harry Sonneborn had an idea to make McDonald's more money and create a better image with financial institutions, Kroc listened very carefully. Sonneborn suggested that McDonald's lease or buy potential sites and lease and sublease them to franchisees to secure the financial future of the company. Kroc opened his ears, and McDonald's became more than a burger company; it was now in real-estate too.

Listen without Ego

Kroc utilised standardisation to make sure that every burger would taste the same, whether a person was eating in New York, London, or Tokyo. He also made "Quality, Service, Cleanliness, and Value," the foundation of the company. This application of WOW required intense dedication to the fine details. Employees were not allowed to flip a burger: they had to turn it. He also insisted that all burgers and fries were to be binned if they weren't bought within minutes of being cooked.

Kroc shook up the world of franchising, but he was flexible enough to allow franchisees to decide the best method to market McDonald's products. It was a Californian franchisee who created Ronald McDonald, and Kroc loved the idea. He knew that children would ask their parents and grandparents to take them to McDonald's, and it would grow as a family restaurant. Ronald McDonald appeared in his first TV advert in 1965, and within six years, 96% of children in America could identify the clown before their president.

It was a franchisee from Cincinnati who put fish on the menu because every Catholic customer wouldn't eat meat on Fridays. Kroc hated the fish idea at first because he thought it would create the wrong smell for the restaurant. However, he listened carefully to the truth and changed his mind. Kroc also opened his ears and mind to the wisdom of the man he treated like a son. Fred Turner was a former shoe salesman and the son of a biscuit salesman. He's famous for launching McDonald's Hamburger University in 1961 and writing the company's training manual for managers, franchisees, and employees. He also introduced McDonald's Egg McMuffin and Chicken Nuggets. Kroc stayed ahead of his time by listening to Turner.

He knew that when you listen you

- get time to understand and evaluate your priorities.

- allow for errors in understanding to be rectified.

- hear the words that indicate a company and a career are in a state of paralysis – An example is, "We have our own way of doing things."

Listen Truthfully

If you wish to discover the truth in a conversation, you must ask what level you listen on. Do you

- listen with a pretend head nod?

- listen, but generalise, distort, and delete information that doesn't suit you?

- listen with prejudice?

- listen openly and honestly with respect and a determination to learn?

☐   listen openly and honestly with respect and a determination to learn and authentically respond?

> *"There's a lot of difference between listening and hearing."*
>
> **G.K. Chesterton**

Responsive Listening

When you respond to today's customer, it's advisable to pause after they speak. If you jump in and interrupt them, you signal that you probably are not listening as you should do. You should also demonstrate an understanding of what you heard to verify your authenticity. You can start your response with words like

☐   "It sounds like,"

☐   "So, you're saying,"

☐   "You mean,"

The art of listening is the number-one skill a great salesperson has. It's impossible to communicate effectively if you're not a great listener, and it's impossible to be a great listener if you're not a great thinker. Is the art of listening easy? No, it's not. It takes energy, motivation, and concentration, but it's one of your best communication tools. The biggest barrier between two people is their inability to listen intelligently, understandingly, and skilfully. Ralph Waldo Emerson said, "The whole course of things goes to teach us faith. We need only obey. There is guidance for each of us, and by lowly listening we shall hear the right word...."

WOW Listening

A WOW listener is careful not to judge, but understands we all have the ability to say the wrong thing at the wrong time. A WOW listener won't generalise, distort, or delete any information they receive. They use it to ask a clarifying question when the opportunity arises. A WOW listener doesn't wander in thought, but strives to understand everything in full. A WOW listener is calm and curious and not affected by differences in personality or delivery styles. A WOW listener learns about today's customer's needs and wants and discovers when they're ready to accept an offer of value.

If you look at past interviews on Michael Parkinson's talk shows on the BBC, you'll see that it was his powerful listening skills that allowed him to ask relevant questions, which allowed his guests to open up. Legendary American talk show host Larry King proclaimed that attentive listening allowed him to choose his next question. This was better than having a standard formula of questions that bored his guests. Listening with good intention makes today's customer or any listener feel unique. Isn't it worth doing it properly?

*"Luck meets us all
in some way.
Listen up.
Can you hear it coming
your way?"*

Darren Kelly

The Listening Company

McDonald's prides itself today on being a company that listens. The value of customer understanding is instilled in every course at Hamburger University. McDonald's customer communication strategy is best in class. The company that gave the world the Quarter Pounder in 1973 evolves continually. Ray Kroc would've loved the launch of the new McWrap and the Blueberry Pomegranate Smoothie in 2013. That's because he knew that a company must successfully adapt its offering for an ever evolving customer. Today's customer can increase your sales if you listen to them. McDonald's cleverly evolves by using customer feedback from authentic conversations offline and online. It's highly regarded for opening the doors of its world-renowned supply chain. You must look at the *What makes McDonald's?* videos on YouTube. They're a lesson in corporate social responsibility and customer engagement for any company.

Have you ever wondered how McDonald's makes its chicken nuggets, or what you can eat if you're a diabetic? You must look at *See Your Questions Answered* on www.mcdonalds.com. You're actually encouraged to ask any possible question about McDonald's food and its supply chain. In return, you'll receive honest replies from truthful employees. However, it's not just the menu that evolves. Have you noticed that many McDonald's restaurants have been transformed, with the bright red décor making way for a deep green? This natural and softer look supports McDonald's green practices. They include the conversion of used oil into biodiesel fuel for the company's transportation needs.

You and your company must listen like McDonald's. Listening helps you adapt more quickly to sell your products and services in any market or any economic situation. *Forbes* magazine called McDonald's the world's sixth *Most Valuable Brand* in 2013. McDonald's reported in 2013 that it employs over 1.8 million people globally and serves food and drink to over 68 million customers every day in 119 countries. You won't reach the success you desire without putting today's customer first. You can only put them first if you listen to them.

HELLO PROFIT Challenge 4

A Plan with Ears

A rigid five-year plan creates a laugh today because most plans must accommodate stakeholder impatience. The rules of today are plan, act, revise, act, revise, act, and do it fast. You don't have the luxury of a tortoise like crawl to success. You need to be fast, flexible, and fluid to be fantastic. To succeed, you must have a plan with ears – one that can help you adapt on the move.

A plan with ears contains the best short-term and long-term strategies. If a plan is short-term only, you reduce your decision making process to being purely reactive. If it's long-term only, you can become complacent with future dreams while current challenges choke your growth.

You must be analytical and exact when you plan. There's a difference between a desire to increase sales within three months and a total commitment to increase sales by 15% within three months.

- What do you want to achieve now?
- What do you want to achieve next week?
- What do you want to achieve this month?
- What do you want to achieve a year from now?

- What do you want to achieve in five years' time? You mustn't speak in terms of "I'd like to." Please commit to using words like, "I must, I will, or I can."

- Here's the biggest question of them all. Why do you want to achieve what's on your list?

- How will you complete your plan? What resources do you possess, and what resources do you need?

- What's the most effective and efficient way to obtain these resources?

- What are your weakest areas, and what training do you need to resolve any problems in these areas? McDonald's has overtaken the American Army as the world's largest trainer of employees because they believe that their employees must be trained, motivated, and re-energised to achieve peak performance for peak profitability.

- How will you monitor the value of your plan on a daily, weekly, and monthly basis?

- Recessions, politics, changes of law, today's customer's preferences, and finances can play a part in destroying your plan. How will you remain agile? Who will you listen to? What will you read? What industry body will you pay most attention to? Who are the experts in your field that you admire?

- Can your expertise be transferred to an emerging market that could offer you a more profitable yield?

❐ What are your conversion ratios for customer interactions? How many interactions does it take for them to buy? How can you improve these figures?

Keep your plan visible, read it every day, and measure your success against your targets. You've now created your plan and analysed reality. You must set your plan in motion. But keep your ears open like Kroc did. You may just discover a valuable shortcut to success. Your plan with ears will always help you sell with WOW.

5. Sharing for Success

"Why cannot they share their tools and thus increase each other's working powers? Indeed they must do so or else the temple may not be built, or, being built, it may collapse."

Winston Churchill

- ☐ Trust and Value
- ☐ Sharing with Purpose
- ☐ 3S Internal Sharing ™
- ☐ Avoid a Concrete Culture
- ☐ Sharing for Change
- ☐ Kelly's Lucky Message ™
- ☐ Formula for Speed
- ☐ Skill Up for Sharing

- ☐ **HELLO PROFIT Challenge 5**

   The Team Player

Trust and Value

You can't sell with WOW unless you share success in your company. Sharing is the act of giving something to another person or persons. I'm surprised by the number of salespeople who say they're not fond of sharing successful ideas, insights, and strategies with their team. How can any salesperson not want to share success with like-minded progressive people? A remarkable thing happens when the intellectual and emotional firepower of different people share success – high profit sales. It's the route to sustaining a powerful company.

Sharing builds business and personal friendships that support each other. But you must earn the right for help by helping other people in your company get what they want first. Sharing isn't about calculation: it's about trust and value to develop *One-Company*: a group of people who create an enriching work environment and WOW customer experiences through their communications. This chapter will show you how and why the power of *One-Company* is essential for WOW.

Sharing with Purpose

One of the world's most successful leaders is a master at sharing. Indra Nooyi is the Chairperson of the Board and CEO of PepsiCo. She was born in Chennai, Tamil Nadu, India in 1955. *Fortune* magazine called her the most powerful businesswoman in the world from 2006 to 2010. Nooyi is the daughter of a male banker and the granddaughter of a male district judge. She holds a Bachelor's degree in Chemistry from Madra Christian College and a Post-Graduate Diploma in Business Administration from the Indian Institute of Management, Calcutta. Nooyi moved to America in 1978 to pursue her MBA at Yale. Her career began as a strategy consultant for the Boston Consulting Group. Her journey took her to PepsiCo in 2000 where she became CFO. By 2006, her success was recognised when she was offered the position of CEO.

Nooyi's mantra is "performance with purpose," and she uses this mantra to prove that people and the planet can work in harmony to create profit. Nooyi includes employees, today's customer, associates, external partners, and the communities that PepsiCo serves. Why does Nooyi care so much about people and why they should live and work with purpose? She was involved in a life-threatening car accident in the eighties, so maybe her brush with death inspires her to appreciate every day.

When Nooyi became CEO of PepsiCo, she put her ego aside and embraced her rival for the top job. She persuaded him to stay with the company by upgrading his role. By doing this Nooyi improved morale, kept her best team together, and saved time on the job of finding a new deputy. Nooyi succeeded by using her intelligence and her deep understanding of human nature. In an interview with the BBC, she revealed that she calls her mother in India twice a day. Nooyi said you must never forget you're a person, a mother, a wife, and a daughter.

Nooyi shows you that great companies are built on honest humanity that doesn't hide and hoard excellence. Time is saved when a salesperson loses their ego and invites other internal expertise to support them. It fosters a deeper sense of living the company brand from the inside out. A salesperson who hides and hoards information, and builds departmental walls that create turf wars deprives their company of valuable resources. They also deprive today's customer of a truly integrated solution from a company of one team.

A company must have a culture that shares information across rank and file, and across location. Sales departments must speak to marketing and to finance and to every other department that supports integrated systems for outstanding customer experiences. This reduces repetition and duplication and saves you, your company, and today's customer precious time and money.

> *"Am I not destroying my enemies when I make friends of them?"*
>
> Abraham Lincoln

3S Internal Sharing ™

Simplify, Standardise, and Support

Does your company's internal communication strategy for today's customer simplify, standardise, and support information integration? Many companies seem to think that a CRM (Customer Relationship Management) system is only a piece of technology, when in fact, it's a crucial part of a company's business plan. It offers a support to store, measure, and make relevant business sense of organised information. But problems arise when it's not integrated and made relevant for today's customer's needs and wants. I know of one company that hounded a customer for an unpaid bill of £2,500. An integrated CRM system would have revealed the customer had never missed a payment before and was about to sign a new contract worth £450,000. This unnecessary harassment showed how CRM must be integrated across departments.

Can you answer the following questions?

- ☐ Does your CRM integrate every customer touching point, so that any problems can be looked at from an overall picture of the relationship?

- ☐ Do you look at previous transactions, but not have details of the latest or upcoming contract?

- ☐ Does your CRM system create departmental partnerships or walls?

- ☐ How much does that cost you?

- ☐ Does every department update all new information immediately?

- ☐ Who loves you?

- ☐ Who loathes you?

- ☐ Why?

- ☐ When do they buy?

- ☐ What do they spend?

- ☐ On what day do they buy the most?

- ☐ What's the average budget of every customer?

- ☐ What are they saying about you online, or to another customer?

You must be able to track today's customer's journey with your company, so you can understand their growing needs and wants. You need to know if you can offer a discount, preferential payment terms, or other concessions. Their track record and future plans will help you decide. You can also use this information to prevent price erosion. Your CRM may tell you today's customer was happy with previous interactions. You can use that as your company's selling point. If you say your company is great that may be true, but if today's customer has said it, it's undeniably true. That's what I call a moment of **WOW**.

However, a lapse in **WOW** values for customer care can reduce this technology's value to that of a poor filing system. There must be a coming together of human and computer intelligence for a **CRM** system to work. Assign someone to manage your CRM system, so they can protect the information, update it with relevance, and support you in your bid to create lifetime value for today's customer. This person can protect an average salesperson from giving away information that may make them sound intrusive, e.g. "I see Mrs Nooyi you told my colleague John in 2002 that you stopped playing the guitar in 1999." There's being friendly, and there's being overfamiliar and weird! Only use the information you need to serve and sell with **WOW**.

Ineffective internal and external communication can have a terrible effect on profit. When relationships break down you inevitably suffer the cost caused by

- negativity.

- unimportant and repetitive conversations.

- ineffective and tedious meetings.

- ☐ people taking undue credit for other people's work.

- ☐ people delivering unfair blame.

- ☐ information not shared in a timely manner.

- ☐ people hiding the truth.

- ☐ absenteeism.

How much do all these things cost you and your company? It doesn't have to be this way! You may never eliminate them, but you can easily reduce them.

Avoid a Concrete Culture

Sales managers must develop agile teams and not blinkered solo salespeople. I spoke to a sales manager of a *Fortune 500* company in 2012. I asked him about his best salesperson and how he rewarded him beyond salary and commissions. His answer included everything from holidays to iPads. I asked him about what this salesperson did that was different from the rest of the team. He told me the salesperson stayed close to the marketing department and used their marketing skills in his customer communication. He accessed the latest surveys, press releases, and PR, and he used them in his presentations and weekly updates for his customer base. I asked the sales manager what would've happened if this salesperson had shared his skills and wisdom with the team and if the others supported him in return. I said, "How would that have affected overall sales?" The change in the sales manager's expression was startling.

Any company can sell if the selling is reactive, but ongoing proactive selling is where the real profit is. You can't have a culture of ongoing proactive selling if you don't create a culture of teamwork. I know this is an alien concept for many companies and professional services firms, but the money squandered every year is simply disgraceful. Every salesperson must lose their solo policy and seek support from their colleagues. They must also introduce their colleagues to their customer base. If today's customer is connected to a company at more than one level, it strengthens the bond. A formidable team also saves time in preparing for a new customer when one of the team has already solidified a great relationship with the customer. It's common sense; don't you think?

Sharing for Change

Many companies have salespeople who like doing things the way they've always been done. They become concrete communication blocks in their company and they play the game to get by. They obstruct WOW. These salespeople need to adapt, but they must face their reasons for their reluctance to change first.

- ☐ Are they stuck in a familiar zone?

- ☐ Are they being guided by historical errors?

- ☐ Are they demotivated?

- ☐ Do they feel that change will destroy their confidence?

When Charles Darwin wrote *The Origin of Species,* his work attacked the foundations of natural history and respected science and religion. Many people didn't like his work because it forced them to think their beliefs about life were wrong all along. However, change should never be thought of as an admission that you're wrong. It should be part of an acceptance that the world is changing constantly, so you must change constantly if only to stay the same.

Indra Nooyi turned PepsiCo from a recognised manufacturer of junk food to a brand that offers today's customer healthy options like Tropicana and Quaker Oats. She understands change is an "essential step in PepsiCo's journey to continue to deliver sustainable growth." Obesity is turning sugar into the new cigarette. Sugar is addictive and partly responsible for heart disease; the number one killer in the world. Nooyi must be given credit for her ability to address a global problem while driving business growth. However, many salespeople and leaders

- remain in denial about change.
- believe in change, but think it's for other people and not them.
- wait for a perfect time to change.
- think change is a one-off.

The main reason many companies stumble through periods of change is because the urgency of the change is clogged with poor internal communication. This creates a personal survival mentality when in fact; a shared ownership mentality is needed for WOW. A dictatorial top down communication style for leading change can lead to whispers of discontent and anti-leadership feelings. Nooyi prefers the Socratic style of engagement – decisive questions that encourage dialogue, even if they're divisive at first. Every employee must be included and respected in a discussion for change. This offers employees a sense that they're valued. It leads to greater motivation and production. If a leader won't listen or respond to feedback they'll encourage their employees to lie to them. A company with such dishonesty can never hope to change and flourish as it should do.

However, open communication for change is open to many dangers. Some members of a management team can take information from a leader personally and reinterpret it to suit their department's needs and wants. This can create conflict and departmental walls. A leader must ensure their management team believe and appreciate a united message by using a form of communication called *Kelly's Lucky Message* ™.

Kelly's Lucky Message ™

Lucky

- **Listen** - Prepare the way for concentrated listening. Isn't it true that a message received during a time of excitement or during a time of stress will have a different effect on the receiver? Set the perfect scene for concentrated and unselfish listening. You can't always set the perfect scene because people communicate on the move, so I suggest you encourage time for concentrated listening. If you send an important message to an employee and they glance at it, scan it, or listen to it without understanding it, your message is wasted.

- **Understand** - Ensure your message is easily understood. Think about the language of each audience. Is the language your audience's first language? What's the best way to communicate? Should it be face-to-face, email, text, video etc.?

- **Challenge** - Ask for feedback, but guide the feedback to support your team. The management team should offer choices or challenges that encourage feedback. A great question is 'What if?' Discussions like this can help a leader discover if his intuition about a piece of information is really a hidden prejudice.

- **Kindle** – The word kindle means to set something on fire. A leader must use the inspired consensus decision to kindle a glowing unity and communicate the new message with a burning passion for progress and results.

- **Yes** - After final acceptance, everyone must agree on the implementation date.

Once agreement is reached at management level, a leader must ensure their message is delivered for feedback throughout the company. This part of the process is prone to errors even if management are completely on board. A leader must ask these questions about each management member.

Top Down

- How will they communicate the information to their team without distorting it or creating message overload?

- How will they make the message relevant and personal to each department while uniting and empowering the company as a whole?

- How will they ensure all employees feel comfortable giving feedback without fearing for their jobs or prospects?

5. Sharing for Success

☐ Do they have the confidence to accept feedback from dissenting voices?

☐ Can they challenge erroneous opinions with empathy and clarity?

☐ How will they tackle faulty assumptions based on previously misunderstood information?

Bottom Up

Once the message has been delivered downwards it must be discussed at the top again. This process is prone to problems too. A leader must ask the following questions.

☐ Is the management team's information varnished in any way?

☐ Is the management team intellectually and emotionally equipped to communicate information upwards with clarity and empathy?

☐ Does the management team have supportive and reliable evidence for any information it offers?

☐ How is the frontline represented in the final decision?

☐ (As a leader) Am I ready to listen to the truth without my ego generalising, devaluing, or distorting any information through select or prejudiced listening?

Employees won't adopt and integrate deep change by being told what to do. If they're not sold, the true cost of such poor communication may only be discovered when it's too late.

Formula for Speed

One of the best examples of a company that lives and breathes a sharing strategy is the Yorkshire based LNT Group. Its founding Chairman is Lawrence Tomlinson, a man with an estimated fortune of over £500 million. LNT Group employs over 2000 people across its five diverse core businesses; Ideal Care Homes, LNT Construction, LNT Software, LNT Solutions and Ginetta. It's easy for a company to express its values, but living them is the real challenge. Tomlinson, a true cultural guardian and innovator, has created a company that moves as smoothly and as swiftly as the Ginetta motor cars it manufactures. His employees

- know where the company is going.

- receive financial, intellectual, and emotional support for their projects.

- receive expert training.

- are encouraged to be innovative.

- are supported to serve every customer ethically.

- enjoy opportunities for career advancement.

Tomlinson told me that he bought every one of his employees an iPhone. This means they're all able to access the same apps and no one is ever stuck for a phone charger! Tomlinson sends his employees video messages about the group's performance. This means that every person from the cooks in Ideal Care Homes to the engineers at LNT Software can access his messages immediately and respond directly to him. Today's smartphone is now the central point for our communication. We don't have to be tied to our desks or have to wait for a laptop to boot up. Tomlinson's innovative style shows how *Lucky* works in his company with a direct leader to employee message. He communicates his messages in the most efficient and easily digestible mode for his employees. His messages are clear and inspiring, so no one is left wondering what he means. His honesty promotes group honesty, so employees feel they can challenge or suggest ideas easily and productively. He said, "We take pride in being a listening company. Every iPhone has a "contact Lawrence" button on the iLNT app, so I get immediate and honest feedback." Tomlinson feeds all new information back to his employees and ensures everyone is on board as the group moves forward with final decisions.

Tomlinson knows every employee and it's obvious from my time in his company that they enjoy his presence and support. He has built a two way trust factor with his employees that promotes the group's values of quality, value, and innovation. When you combine that with the fact that every employee is a shareholder in the group, you know your team is progressive and unified. Tomlinson wins because he acts with care. LNT Group shows other companies that they must place communication at the core of their company. Every employee must know their role in their company and the results required for reward. Command and control will never inspire employees to volunteer their hearts and minds to their work. Inspiring and motivating employees require dedication; the sort that helped the multi-talented Tomlinson come first in the GT2 class of the Le Mans 24 hour race in 2006.

> *"It takes two flints to make a fire."*
>
> **Louisa May Alcott**

Skill Up for Sharing

When Indra Nooyi spoke at the 2011 Commencement address at Wake Forest University, she took her audience back to 1986. She was working for the Boston Consulting Group as Head of Strategy for the automotive electronics division of Motorola. Nooyi wanted to be able to communicate with and understand a team of engineers. She revealed that she studied from 7 a.m. to 9 a.m., four mornings every week to learn about electronics and cars. Nooyi admitted the work was hard, but she felt empowered by contributing more. Nooyi is an excellent example of a leader who takes time to share and serve within her own company.

Nooyi understands that a company must communicate in a holistic and honest manner. That communication must be intelligent and emotional if it seeks to succeed. When you make an effort to communicate with today's customer through the prism of teamwork, you break down barriers to speed up the flow of solutions.

I think every company should heed the advice of Richard Branson and have a Director of Fun. Branson suggests that the role should include responsibility for organising events like concerts and nightclub events. Is it any wonder that Branson is regarded as a business hero by so many people? Like Lawrence Tomlinson, he gets it; when you adopt an attitude of fun you create transparency. When you enjoy transparency, you develop trust. When you develop trust, you inspire talent. When you inspire talent, you create WOW teamwork.

In Malcolm Walker's brilliant book *Best Served Cold* he revealed how he chartered three jumbo jets to take over 1,000 of his employees to Disney World, Florida. The whole event cost over £4 million, but it inspired his company to achieve record profits. The Iceland Foods CEO made the point that happy employees make a happy environment for a happy customer, who will always spend more and more often. It's evident that Walker understands and knows how to sell with WOW. Is it any surprise that Iceland Foods was awarded *The Sunday Times Best Big Company to Work For* in the UK in 2012 and 2014?

HELLO PROFIT Challenge 5

The Team Player

You must be a team player if you wish to succeed because if your team fails, you may fail. Wouldn't life be so much easier if you knew your team believed, respected, understood, and supported you? Before you expect that level of team spirit ask if you play your part. If you don't play your part, you may receive no support when your biggest challenges arise. You may also find that you'll have no one to share your greatest triumphs with too. Ask the following questions to gauge if you generate WOW teamwork in your company.

- ☐ When was the last time I said "sorry" to a colleague and meant it?

- ☐ When was the last time I accepted a colleague's apology gracefully?

- ☐ When was the last time I shared a new discovery that helped my team?

- ☐ When was the last time I supported an outside working hours team initiative, like a charity event or social gathering?

- ☐ Have I ever grumbled the words, "That's not my job" when my colleagues needed support?

☐ When was the last time I provided a solution for a team problem?

☐ Do I honestly know my role and responsibilities in my team?

☐ Do I know my strengths in my team, and do I accept my weaknesses?

☐ Am I close enough to my colleagues to know what motivates them, so I can communicate with them more effectively?

☐ Do I inspire my team with a positive attitude in everything I say and do?

☐ Do I recognise the specialists in my team, and how they can support my team and me?

☐ Do I give my full support to my team until every unique challenge reaches the best possible conclusion?

6. Network for Net Worth

*"The only way to have a friend
is to be one."*

Ralph Waldo Emerson

- [ ] A World Champion Hello
- [ ] Golden Phone Calls
- [ ] Ear Catching Voicemail
- [ ] The Valued Call
- [ ] Link up on LinkedIn
- [ ] Be a Twit
- [ ] Engage with Email
- [ ] **HELLO PROFIT Challenge 6**

    Net Worth Generator

A World Champion Hello

You can't sell with WOW unless you network. Networking is the art of authentically developing supportive relationships. Some people say, "It's not what you know, but who you know." Other people say, "It's not who you know, but what you know about who you know." I like the words of Brian Tracy. He is to sales training what Ali was to boxing – the greatest. He said, "Successful people are always looking for opportunities to help others." You must follow that principle if you want to build your network to increase your net worth (net assets). A person in a network who puts other people first with truth and value is easy to recognise.

In 2004, I met a hero of mine at *The Irish Post Awards* in London to celebrate Irish success worldwide. This was a WOW moment for me. I couldn't believe my luck when I sat beside the former WBA featherweight champion and member of the International Boxing Hall of Fame. Barry McGuigan, MBE was born on 28 February, 1961 in Clones, Ireland. I can easily recall the night I watched him defeat the reigning WBA featherweight champion, Eusebio Pedroza of Panama at Loftus Road, London in 1985.

McGuigan writes a popular boxing column and he commentates all over the world. His other work includes his choreography and editing expertise for all the boxing scenes for the Golden Globe nominated movie *The Boxer*. He also trained its star Daniel Day Lewis for the movie. McGuigan is liked, respected, and trusted by many people in business and sport. From the moment I met McGuigan he was a perfect gentleman. When I approached our table he stood up, offered me a handshake first, and beamed a welcoming smile. I'll explain the lessons a world champion can offer to help you nourish every relationship you enjoy, and wish to create.

- ☐ He asked many questions about me, which showed he's genuinely interested in other people.

- ☐ He only spoke about himself when I asked.

- ☐ He only offered advice after seeking permission to give it.

- ☐ He included everyone at the table in the conversation.

- ☐ He didn't look around the room to see who was watching. Too many people look around to see if someone else is more appealing or beneficial to them.

- ☐ He was honest. He told me how he handled his fears and challenges inside and outside the ring.

- ☐ He listened to my words on boxing as though they were as respected as his words.

- ☐ He possessed a delightful sense of humour. He could laugh at himself easily.

- ☐ He was a master storyteller. When he told me about the night at Loftus road in 1985, it was almost like I was sitting ringside. I could almost hear the pounding punches, see and smell his face drip with sweat, and feel the influence of the crowd's thunderous chants.

- ☐ He was confident yet humble.

I suggest you save your selling pitch for when you need it. Don't come across as a self-serving salesperson. If you're new to sharing value, please pay attention to the wisdom of a boxing champion and some additional rules.

- ☐ Reach out to new people and don't just hover over the buffet with your best friends.

- ☐ Encourage other people to give their views and tell their stories.

- ☐ Respect other people's skills and judgements and learn from them.

- ☐ Remember people's names.

- ☐ Never be unfairly negative. People don't need another Moaning Minnie in their lives.

- ☐ Go outside your current group and introduce someone new, so they feel welcome.

- ☐ Thank the people who shared their stories and wisdom. Your interest, warmth, and enthusiasm will be remembered.

- ☐ Do it regularly to build relationships.

- ☐ Speak about things that interest other people.

- ☐ No one likes to be told they're wrong, so don't tell them. Lead them to the truth instead.

- ☐ Look at things through other people's viewpoints.

☐ Follow up your conversations with value and concern instead of just placing your recently collected business cards in your drawer. Make sure you follow up within 24 hours. Don't worry if other people don't follow up. You must establish and keep your own high standards in line with your WOW values.

☐ Treat people with fairness and truthfulness.

☐ Invite people to one of your company's events.

☐ Offer value that's practical and timely.

> *"If I have seen further than others, it is by standing upon the shoulders of giants."*
>
> **Isaac Newton**

Golden Phone Calls

One of the toughest places to share your expertise with today's customer is on the phone, but it's a medium we all must use. Isn't it true that you and your team will make or answer phone calls every day? These calls may be a follow-up to a warm lead, an introductions lead, prospect calls, or inbound queries. Isn't it also true that you'll often hear, "I'm not interested," "We already have a supplier," "Just send me the information," or "I don't understand"?

Would you like to know why a great salesperson rarely hears these words? It's because they understand the secrets of WOW for phone success. An average salesperson feels frustrated when they jump hurdles to reach a decision maker only to lose rapport within the first 10 seconds of the call. They also feel further frustration when they get past the first 10 seconds only to send today's customer into indifference. I know a great salesperson who calls his phone, "The Golden Phone." He imagines that every phone call he makes is with a golden phone. He uses this image to help him internalise the belief that every conversation he has by phone can build his success. His phone calls today are the type you would love to receive. They're warm, authentic, entertaining, and relevant, and focused on today's customer's needs and wants. Compare his belief with an average salesperson who fears making a phone call, or one who's arrogant, uninformed, or boring.

Phone calls are used to sell, to set up a meeting, to gather enough relevant information for a better follow up call, or to care for an unsatisfied customer. Even when a phone call is engaging, an average salesperson destroys any chance of future business. That's because they fail to discover the information that will make their meeting or follow-up phone call even better. Let's discover if you've ever been a victim of such ineffectiveness. Have you ever received the same call with the same boring script from an average salesperson a few weeks apart? Did they believe that a time lapse would make you more willing to listen? Did you feel offended by their attempt to annoy you into submission? A great salesperson does something that powers their success and builds authentic relationships: they put themselves in today's customer's shoes.

Many people say that practice makes perfect, but this isn't so. Only perfect practice makes perfect! If you continue to practice destructive habits, you'll most likely not improve at all. In fact, you'll probably sound more ineffective with every call you make, and you'll wonder why your success is sporadic. You must think, listen, and speak with intention, intensity, and empathy. You must know how to open a conversation, qualify effectively, and achieve results.

A great salesperson knows that a brand is a cluster of logical and emotional attachments to today's customer. Every phone interaction either builds your brand or hurts its status. The moment you ask for a second of today's customer's time you're either adding value or wasting their time. There's nothing in between. So you must ask yourself if your phone conversations are simply marketing monologues or magical conversations of trust, confidence, and value. If your answer is the former, do you realise how much money, and brand damage these conversations are costing you? The real cost will shock you, but there's a solution. Today's customer is conditioned by boring, robotic, and information heavy phone calls. They rarely experience WOW by phone. This means they're programmed to turn you off too. It seems unfair that another salesperson's laziness and poor knowledge can taint your skill and expertise.

You may have seen Nicholas Cage in the movie *Gone in 60 Seconds*. Today's customer may be gone in 10 seconds if you fail to build rapport and connect. Today's customer may not hang up the phone, but their mind may go elsewhere. They may subconsciously think, "I don't like this uninformed or high pressure salesperson, and I don't like them wasting my time," or they may ask, "Why is this person, intruding on my time?" You mustn't make the mistakes that lead today's customer into a negative inner conversation.

Isn't it strange that most people stop thinking when they pick up the phone? I've met many articulate and intelligent people who fall to pieces verbally when they speak on the phone. When you speak, you want the person you call to hear a mature and confident person. It's important to realise that people can hear your smile down the phone line. Don't put on a Cheshire cat grin, but you should adopt a feeling of natural enthusiasm that allows you to flow and pause with warmth. If you sit up straight or stand up, you'll sound more energetic. If you gesticulate as if the person is facing you, you'll give more spice to your voice. This will make you sound more appealing to the person taking your phone call.

The number-one thing that stops a salesperson sounding confident on the phone is the fear of being told, "No," or they're not needed. However, most salespeople defeat themselves before they make a phone call. I'm often asked if I recommend that a salesperson should write scripts to deliver on the phone. I believe that it's better to use a script than sound unfocused. However, you don't want to sound robotic either. You should rehearse your script, so that you sound natural. It sounds strange, but you must rehearse to sound natural. Think about the person you're calling and what the call will do for them and for you. You must capture today's customer's attention and keep it by being interesting and relevant and by remaining focused on the value you offer. These are the golden rules for using the phone.

- Sound confident when you speak to the gatekeeper. "Can I help you?"

    "Yes. Barry please."

    "Who's calling?"

    "Billy John from XYZ."

    If you were referred by someone they know and trust, say, "Helen H suggested I call regarding your company's problem in London." Remember to sell the benefit of the call, or they may not take it.

- Seek permission to engage the other person briefly. This shows you respect them and won't take long. Use a pre-emptive sentence to show you respect their time and want to provide value. "Barry. I know you're busy. This will only take two minutes."

- Make the call about them right to the end.

- Use their first name. Barry is less formal than Mr McGuigan.

- Tell them your name in full.

- Use a hook to get them to listen. "Barry, I helped your competitor increase their sales on average 23% over three years. Would you be interested in finding out how I did it?" Always ask a positive question.

- Prevent misunderstandings with a summary.

- Show manners by allowing today's customer to say the last word.

- Never finish today's customer's sentences for them.

- Avoid any conflict on the phone.

- Introduce a hook to set up a meeting or whatever your next step may be.

- Using a speakerphone is rude because today's customer may feel you're not giving them your full concentration, or someone else is listening.

- Always try to get today's customer's direct line. It makes it easier to reach them.

- Separate your calling time for today's customer. Do all prospect calls together and all current calls together if possible.

- Always reconfirm an appointment.

- There's no perfect time to call. Start calling the minute you arrive at work. The more you put it off the more your motivation drops. Stop making excuses for a sunny Friday afternoon or a wet Monday morning. It's not your decision to make because you can't read today's customer's mind.

- You want to approach today's customer, but you don't want to annoy them. The best way to do this is to support your call with an online message. Send a warm email promising to call.

- Treat the gatekeeper with the same respect as you would give to today's customer. Don't be a lick up and kick down self-centred salesperson. It's not right, and you'll eventually be found out.

- Become a master of the 30-second story, or the metaphor to tell your story clearly and quickly (See more on this subject in chapters seven and ten).

- Don't defeat yourself by thinking you're being pushy. People are exceptionally busy and may appreciate your self-described pushiness as absolute professionalism.

- Visualise success during and after your preparation. An Olympic champion wins the race in their mind before the race begins. A great salesperson visualises customer appreciation. To visualise success, you must use all the senses to create a picture of your value being appreciated.

- Never hang up abruptly.

Ear Catching Voicemail

Have you ever started to leave a voicemail message and lost your train of thought? It's not a nice feeling because there's no way to erase your message and start again. A poor message can make you sound incompetent at best. Listen to the messages on your voicemail and think about which ones are clear and purposeful, but still grab your attention. Which ones gave you a compelling reason to call a person back? Think about the purpose of your voicemail? Is it to seek a request or to deliver information?

Here are the golden rules for leaving a voicemail.

- Say today's customer's name first and at least one more time during your message.

- Don't overwhelm them with a message that tries to use up the memory on their phone. Keep your message to 15-seconds max.

- Say your phone number twice and slowly.

- Mention an issue they discussed and a solution you have. "Hi Barry. Billy John here from XYZ. It was lovely to speak to you yesterday. I thought about your problem regarding X, and I just might have the solution for you. I can explain it in two minutes Barry. I'm on 00X000076000. That's 00X000076000. Take care."

- Keep your voicemail message free of fillers and crutches, like, "I'm just calling to see."

- If you've never left a concise voicemail message before, I suggest you write one. It's better to deliver a competent and relevant message, as opposed to sounding like you've just seen a ghost.

☐ Don't give your solution in the message. Otherwise, today's customer may have no reason to call you back.

☐ Don't restrict today's customer to a time to call you back. It's another pressure in their busy schedule.

☐ Voicemail works best before 10am because today's customer has the day to call you.

An average salesperson communicates from their own selfish mindset, so please remember what I said about developing your WOW values in chapter two. If you develop your WOW values, you'll automatically think about today's customer first, and the above techniques will become a natural part of you.

The Valued Call

If you value today's customer, you'll reveal this attitude when you take their call.

☐ Answer the call within four rings.

☐ If the call is put through to you, take it if you can. Say you're busy if you really are.

☐ If you promise to call back, do. Don't play today's customer for a fool by having someone say you're in a meeting if you're not. Think about what this does. You're asking someone on your team to lie for you. This is unfair, but it also creates a culture of deceit in your company. When you ask someone to lie for you, do you seriously think they'll ever trust you again? If trust is one of your WOW values, you must stop the spread of deceit.

- Be respectful and listen carefully to understand.

- Never leave today's customer on hold for longer than 16 seconds. I know these rules are broken by call centres that regard today's customer as a number. I trust you want better than that for today's customer. A leading bank revealed in 2011 that it forgot about its customer base. I wondered how any company could be so foolish. If there's no customer, there's no business. If your interaction with today's customer is by phone, you must get it right every time.

- Use today's customer's name when you say goodbye. It's the most precious word in their vocabulary.

Think about your WOW values for putting today's customer first and adopt the techniques that reflect those values.

Link Up on LinkedIn

A lesson in how to share can be gained by studying the life of LinkedIn co-founder Reid Hoffman. The former Apple and PayPal executive is famous for building talented teams that have included his friends Allen Blue, and Stanford friend Peter Thiel. Hoffman is very much a people person. When Visa threatened to pull the plug on PayPal it was Hoffman's communication skills that bought PayPal the time they needed to survive. After PayPal was sold to eBay Hoffman turned his attention to social sharing for business people. Please bear in mind that the dotcom bubble didn't inspire many people to invest in a new fad called social networking. It wasn't the WOW website it is today. However, Hoffman persisted and soon the veil of secrecy that business people placed over their identity was removed when LinkedIn was founded in 2002. Hoffman recognised the need for people to connect offline because it worked so well for him. It was only natural to take that process online. I believe the following are the most important things for you to consider as you build and amalgamate your online and offline network.

- Complete your profile because it's your online business brand.

- Accept invitations from who you know. Thank people for connecting and make a mutually beneficial suggestion. Don't just accept anyone. They could be your competitors. Do you want your competitors knowing everything about you?

- Personalise every request you make to connect with today's customer.

- How you personalise and start the engagement is crucial. When you connect with anyone, remind them of your shared experience. If they can't remember you, you may be reported for spamming.

- Align with your connections objectives – be relevant.

- Follow today's customer to improve sales intelligence. You can follow their company and gain access to their latest news.

- Contribute to a conversation that today's customer is involved in. Comment on their posts. You'll get more business by paying attention to today's customer's messages of desire than by broadcasting your own. Join targeted industry and local groups to discover people and companies you may serve. Become a thought leader by providing content that's valuable.

- Use "Tags" to segment your connections. You'll discover these in your Contacts. This allows you to send messages to selected people.

- Look at your connections and see who you can connect to other people.

- Ask your connections for introductions.

- Never SPAM! It breaches privacy laws and is rude and inconsiderate.

- Keep your message simple – 88 words max.

- Use advanced searches to reach specific people using seniority, keywords, and key functions.

- Add a video to tell yours or your company's story.

- Have an offensive strategy? Who can you help and who can help you?

- If you wish to see a company's employees' skills go to the top of its LinkedIn company page. Everything you need is in the "Insights" button.

- Use LinkedIn's InMail to guarantee a response for your requested introductions.

☐   Create an enticing subject line and heading for every message.

☐   Search for LinkedIn events such as trade shows. You can introduce yourself to the group and ask them to meet you at the event. A great salesperson fills their day with introductions before they even reach their stand on the day of the event.

☐   Don't try to sell your connections something: it's a turnoff.

☐   Think about your values for putting today's customer first and choose the techniques that reflect those values.

Be a Twit

Twitter is a fabulous tool. It breaks news faster than any other medium. Traditional media uses it for many of its stories. It unites brilliant minds in our immediate world. You can discover what today's customer needs and wants by engaging them and listening to them. You can also correct misconceptions or rectify any errors that have occurred in your service. However, be aware that you should validate your thoughts before you tweet. Think CCS – Craftsmanship, Constraint, and Simplicity.

☐   What do you do? Do you describe it in your bio?

☐   Be positive and honest.

☐   Be relevant, inspiring, and interesting.

☐   Write clear and short tweets that can be understood immediately and hopefully retweeted.

- Help people. Don't invade their space. Comment on their discussion and offer suggestions in a non-pushy way. "Barry. I see you've got a challenge with XYZ. I hope this helps."

- Do it regularly. Timing is crucial. Tweeting about an event that's a week old is too late. We live in an immediate world.

- Add hashtags to your tweets. If your tweet is about Save the Children, put # *Save the Children* in your tweet. It will help people discover your tweet more easily if they search your subject matter.

- It's likely that someone is talking about you or your market today. Use relevant keywords to find these people and join the conversation. See http://hootsuite.com/

- Put your Twitter URL on your email signature and business card. Email and business cards still exist.

- Quality beats quantity in your following. Quality is a result of engagement.

- Share the human side of your company

- Keep your tweets neat. Tiny URL is a terrific shortening tool.

One of the best examples of a company that supports today's customer through Twitter is O2 Ireland. Their use of real time communication helps their customer make decisions in real time. They offer competitions, they offer support, and they sell in a way that offers real time value. They also prove that the ability to support today's customer offline must be supported by an online platform. Twitter is perfect for this aim.

Engage with Email

When you use email, you must create a message that jumps off the screen. Otherwise, it will be scanned briefly and deleted. A powerful message requires brevity with emotional and logical value. A lesson can be learnt from the emotional language that Amazon uses to connect with today's customer. The following words are used by many companies in their communications, but none of them are as consistent as Amazon. Do you use any of the following? "Welcome back, We look forward, …….we wish you the best of luck, Thank you, Please tell us how we are doing, ……thank you, Thanks again, ……best of luck, …….we're thrilled, I hope this helps, Thanks for your understanding, and Did I answer your question?"

In a sales journey, a direct marketing campaign may be used, or a follow-up meeting may be required, and these may involve communication by email. Rapport can be dissolved at this stage by basic errors. Your relationship with today's customer should never be dissolved by a random message in an email. You can't take your words back, so please be extremely careful. Your words will be in text for everyone to see, and in many cases can end up on the internet. Poorly written, emotionally draining, and unintentionally sent emails have destroyed careers.

- ☐ Never send unnecessary emails.

- ☐ Type a great headline, or it may not get opened.

- Avoid lengthy, meandering and unfocused emails. People hate reading emails that don't get to the point. Can you blame them when they may receive hundreds a day? Keep your email brief (90 words max).

- Allow your reader space to understand your message by using paragraph breaks, bullet points, subheadings etc.

- Never get into a disagreement by email. An email can spark a disagreement into a raging fire.

- Avoid humour by email. The greatest comedians have a face that makes us laugh when they make use of humour. You use a white screen and black typed words to promote your humour. What would happen if your email is forwarded to a superior or today's customer who finds it offensive, in terrible taste, or stupid? I offer you the best of luck at your promotion interview!

- Stop your email if the conversation is on the verge of becoming a book. Could the conversation be sorted with a 20-second phone call? Don't waste time trying to write an email while wondering whether your message will be understood? The more the conversation by email grows the greater the chance of miscommunication.

- Never offer poor or irrelevant information. Ask yourself if you're making a valid point, or are you emailing just for the sake of it?

- Never forward confidential emails to others, or CC and BCC just to curry favour. It's not exactly the best way to promote trust and harmony in any team. You also clutter the other person's inbox.

☐ Never list every award you've won in your signature.

HELLO PROFIT Challenge 6

Net Worth Generator

One of the world's biggest selling songs of 2013 was recorded by French duo Daft Punk. It features Pharrell Williams and Chic co-founder, Nile Rodgers. Williams only heard about the project when he met Daft Punk at one of the singer Madonna's parties. Let's look at the ways you can connect with other people to offer your value and friendship. Your authentic desire to help other people will lead to an upsurge in your social profit. Make this your goal and you'll never have to worry about monetary profit.

Use what's useful and relevant to create the top 20 WOW ways you can introduce yourself to your market.

☐ Write a sales letters to a decision maker.

☐ Join your local Chamber of Commerce.

☐ Attend relevant industry seminars.

☐ Give a free consultation or trial.

☐ Speak at a local event.

☐ Speak at a local college.

☐ Attend relevant trade shows.

- ☐ Offer to do charity work.
- ☐ Write a *How to* guide for today's customer.
- ☐ Create a YouTube video to highlight a problem you can solve.
- ☐ Create a podcast that offers today's customer incredible value.
- ☐ Appear in a media interview.
- ☐ Write articles for today's customer's trade magazines.
- ☐ Engage in relevant online conversations.
- ☐ Write a blog that personalises your expertise.
- ☐ Cross promote with a trusted and valued partner.
- ☐ Sit on a panel of experts at a seminar.
- ☐ Write a syndicated column.
- ☐ Write a study of today's customer's business and present it to them.
- ☐ Create a community initiative with like-minded people.
- ☐ Create a business card that contains more than just details. If you can create a card that offers value, today's customer will keep it.
- ☐ Add your thoughts to the comment sections on relevant websites.

PART 2.

7. Belief for Brilliance

8. Rapport for Relationships

9. Wisdom for Winning

10. Passion for Promotion

11. Habit for Harmony

7. Belief for Brilliance

*"Believe and act,
as if it were
impossible to fail."*

Charles F. Kettering

The 20% Principle

- ☐ Activate Self-belief
- ☐ Your True Self
- ☐ Does the Child Rule?
- ☐ No Fear!
- ☐ Reject Rejection
- ☐ Belief beyond University
- ☐ Stimulate Belief
- ☐ Killing Success

The 75% Principle

- [ ] Belief to Communicate
- [ ] Today's Customer's Thinking
- [ ] Belief Warning
- [ ] Kelly's Customer Compass™
- [ ] The Super Confident 30-Second Pitch

The 5% Principle

- [ ] **HELLO PROFIT Challenge 7**

    Meeting Bill
    Meeting Bill again
    10TY (10 Times You)

The 20% Principle

Activate Self-belief

You can't sell with WOW unless you possess WOW self-belief: this means you trust yourself to take successful action. 20% of your success in front of today's customer is related to your self-belief. Isn't it true that today's customer wants to deal with a salesperson who can confidently and expertly help them move forward with their business or personal aims? An average salesperson approaches today's customer with an underlying negative self-belief. They mistakenly believe their negative thinking is really objective thinking: it's not.

You must create positive inner conversations. Words such as "I'm rubbish at that," or, "Why am I so stupid?" have a negative emotional, intellectual, and physical effect on you. They do nothing but cause you harm and destroy your ability to have fun selling. Critical self-analysis is essential for growth, but if your inner voice condemns you to the point of self-defeat, you have a problem.

Sometimes you need to stop being too hard on yourself and appreciate the good you offer the people you serve and lead every day. Ask these questions when you need reminding of how talented and generous you are.

- ☐ In what areas of my life do I create WOW moments?

- ☐ What qualities do I recognise in myself that help other people?

- ☐ What am I most excited about?

- [ ] What subject can I confidently speak about?
- [ ] What successes did I achieve in my life with courage and skill?

Your True Self

Please don't confuse self-belief with arrogance or ignorance. Some people don't care about the truth, while some other people are afraid to hear the truth. They both live their lives in denial. A great salesperson sits somewhere in the middle. They want self-belief that allows them to display their passion, reveal their humility, and create a powerful bond with today's customer.

A salesperson with poor self-belief feels more negatively stressed, is afraid of group communication, and is generally hyper-sensitive to constructive feedback. They find it difficult to clarity their thoughts verbally, and the idea of change frightens them. They also find it hard to apologise and accept an apology. You must believe that you're qualified to provide the solution for today's customer's challenges. You must also believe that you possess the skill and flexibility to adjust to certain objections, disagreements, and distractions that can occur in a conversation with today's customer. If you don't believe you can succeed, then you won't succeed.

Does the Child Rule?

Do you remember when your parents told you not to speak to strangers? I understand they said that to protect you, but isn't the following true. Your partner or best friends were once strangers, and the things you desire now may be in the hands of strangers. A great salesperson rewires their childhood mind to help them connect with strangers and turn them into friends.

Childhood thoughts really can control adult actions. I know one sales leader who avoided speaking in public for 20 years. I discovered that he held a hidden negative belief in his subconscious that people would laugh at him. This negative belief cemented itself in his mind when he was mocked by his school friends on his ninth birthday. His belief formed in his childhood controlled how he felt and acted. I asked him the following questions. "Would you rely on the advice of a nine old with no experience in your field? Are you relying on a self-belief system you developed as a nine year old child?" His answers were "no," and "yes." His honest replies didn't surprise me.

No Fear!

Think about your biggest fears when you engage today's customer. It can be the fear of rejection, the fear of constructive criticism, or the fear of unfair fault finding. These fears can stop you making a phone call, or giving a stand-up presentation, or asking for a decision to buy. Maybe your biggest fear is something else. Many salespeople's fears are hidden in their subconscious minds.

When fears are unobserved, they grow and spread to affect all areas of a salesperson's communication. If you think you've no fears at all, simply think about the jobs you procrastinate over, or the situations you avoid. Think about the times when you decided to commit when the "right moment" arrived. What about a time when you played the blame game and created alibis to back up your excuses. These alibis, or members of the "If only club," may have included weak excuses about your education, family background, age, place of birth, finances, weight, opportunities, the economy, previous failures and your IQ. This self-analysis might seem a little uncomfortable, but the pain caused by unrecognised fears offers you a first class ticket to lesser success than you deserve.

Reject Rejection

The fear of rejection can be more powerful than a salesperson's desire for success. No one likes rejection. So you must reduce the influence of any unfair rejection you face with your own words and thoughts. Epictetus said, "Man is disturbed, not by things, but by the views he takes of them." Your success as a salesperson will be affected by how well you respond to rejection. It doesn't matter how tough you are, the only person who laughs at rejection is part robot. If you're sensitively aware, you'll suffer from the pain of rejection at one point or another in your career. It will catch you when your defences are low through tiredness or pressure. You must always welcome and utilise constructive feedback, but be careful that you don't let rejection smother your belief in yourself. You can easily enter a dangerous world of inner negativity for no reason if you give credence and power to unwanted and unjust rejection.

Isn't it true that all celebrated achievements were rejected and ridiculed at first, then questioned, and then glorified as a piece of brilliance? Did you know that Tina Turner rejected the song *What's love got to do with it* when she heard it first? Did the writers Terry Britten and Graham Lyle get upset, or did they reject Turner's outright rejection? A few changes later and they had a song for Turner that topped the American charts for three weeks in September, 1984. It also won a Grammy for Record of the Year. You must reject rejection and believe that all you may need is a tweak of self-belief to succeed.

Belief beyond University

One great salesperson, who believed he could succeed, changed how we communicate today. Bill Gates was born on 28 October, 1955 in Seattle, Washington. He's a philanthropist and non-executive chairman of Microsoft, which he co-founded with Paul Allen. Gates is also the author of books such as *The Road Ahead*, and *Business @ The Speed of Thought*. He consistently features among the world's richest people, and he topped the list from 1995 to 2007, and again in 2009. He regained the title from Mexico's Carlos Slim in 2013. While at Microsoft, Gates held the position of CEO and Chief Software Architect, and he's still an individual shareholder.

He received criticisms for his business tactics, which some people considered anti-competitive, but his fans will point to the philanthropic enterprises, like The Bill & Melinda Gates Foundation, which supports many charities worldwide. He decided, in 2006, to make the move to work for the Foundation full-time. So what turned this Harvard dropout into what *Fortune* magazine called, the "Sultan of Software"? What possessed him to do things like announce a revolutionary operating system called Windows when it was nowhere near ready? What drove him to change the way the world saw and used computers? The answer lies in the fact that Gates had a vision, and he knew deep inside that success would come his way. It was only a matter of time.

From the moment, Gates read an article about a new microcomputer called *Altair*, in the *Popular Electronics* magazine, he could see the future. He saw the need for new computer software, and his mind exploded with technical possibilities. However, it's wrong to describe Gates as just a technical expert because he's more than that. He's also a smart salesperson who can read others, motivate others, and encourage creative and productive teamwork.

7. Belief for Brilliance

Gates understands the importance of how to sell products, services, and ideas to any audience. He learnt a lot of his selling skills as a child by watching his mother when he accompanied her on her sales visits to various schools across Seattle. In the early days of Microsoft, he made numerous phone calls to sell software to industry giants like Citibank and General Electric. Let's not forget that Gates bought the operating system (86-DOS) from a software company in Seattle and later sold the license to IBM, so they could use it for their new PC's operating system.

When Gates launched Windows 3.0 in 1990, his presentation had an MTV style to it, and this helped the product shift 100,000 copies within two weeks. The Windows 95 launch featured one of America's most popular comedians, Jay Leno, and this helped Microsoft sell over seven million copies of that. Gates understood the art and science of selling. Even his faithful friend Warren Buffet said Gates could become the "Hot Dog King of the World," if that's what he decided to sell.

Stimulate Belief

Gates' TED talk in 2009 on health and education had all the elements of WOW. He showed every salesperson that a demo works wonders to stimulate an audience. To show how frightening the threat of malaria from a mosquito can be he released mosquitoes into the audience. The audience screamed, but the mosquitoes carried no infection. Do you think Gates honest message will ever be forgotten? I'm not advocating the use of insects to empower your communication. I'm simply proving that when you believe in yourself and a cause strongly, your communication is rarely boring and forgetful.

When Microsoft was a young company, Gates said he wanted to see every home and workplace computer running Microsoft's software.

He didn't say he hoped to create software that people could buy if they wanted it. He put the products on the world's computers in his own mind, and that's what a great salesperson does. They already know the outcome of their desires. Current estimates suggest that Microsoft's Windows or at least one of its products such as Windows Media Player or Office operate on over 90% of the world's personal computers.

> *"If you have no confidence in self, you are twice defeated in the race of life. With confidence, you have won even before you have started."*
>
> **Cicero**

Killing Success

Let's look at another killer of self-belief; fear of success. This fear can do as much damage as fear of failure. If you believe that success will have a negative effect on your life, you'll subconsciously say and do things that will restrict your progress. Some average salespeople believe that success will kill their happiness and ruin their personal lives. That shouldn't happen if they possess the zest for achievement and the WOW values I discussed in chapter two.

> *"I saw the angel in the marble and carved until I set him free."*
>
> **Michelangelo**

The 75% Principle

Belief to Communicate

You must be optimistic, but legitimate self-confidence can only be expected after incisive preparation. 75% of your confidence in front of today's customer is related to your understanding of the facts, how they relate to the value you offer, and how you communicate that offer. The Hollywood actor Will Smith is most famous for his TV role as Will in *The Fresh Prince of Bel-Air*. In the nineties, Smith was so dedicated to his profession that he learnt the other actor's lines: that's WOW preparation. An average salesperson prepares and rehearses their lines. A great salesperson creates WOW by using their intellectual and emotional intelligence to anticipate the thoughts and words of today's customer also. The first thing to remember is that you must never assume anything.

Never assume

☐ you know the number-one reason today's customer should buy.

☐ today's customer will make a similar decision to their last one.

☐ today's customer has the answers to their key issues.

☐ internal challenges (redundancies, budget allocations, etc.) can't sabotage your offer at any stage.

☐ external influences (government policies, natural crises, etc.) can't change today's customer's strategy.

- the person with the title makes the final decision.
- your competition isn't planning to offer today's customer WOW products and services.

Today's Customer's Thinking

Today's customer may not buy from you, or deal with you because they

- fear making a bad decision they can't change.
- fear being taken advantage of.
- fear a better WOW deal is available elsewhere.
- are confused by too many choices.
- believe their need isn't urgent.
- are happy with their current supplier.
- fail to understand or accept their problems.
- are bored by your message.
- don't value your products and services.
- desire greater social proof.
- think they've no time.
- think you're too big, too small, too specialised, too general or some other "too."

- [ ] have no budget.

- [ ] are lazy and unmotivated.

You'll find that your conscious and subconscious strategy for taking action is similar to today's customer's strategy. They'll ask the following questions.

- [ ] Do we have a problem?

- [ ] Can we solve it ourselves? No, we can't.

- [ ] Who can supply us with the solution?

- [ ] Does the analysis of the potential supplier match our values and demands?

- [ ] Shall we engage in a relationship with them?

- [ ] What's the best value we can get?

- [ ] Will working with, or buying from these people make us money, save us time, reduce our efforts, and be a trouble-free experience?

- [ ] Shall we offer them repeat business?

When you prepare for today's customer, you should let your mind loose with ideas and questions. When you remove inner criticism for your suggestions at the preparation stage, you may find yourself sneaking up on a solution for today's customer's challenges. This requires you to be at your creative best. Creativity in this case is the process of discovering a better way to solve today's customer's challenges. If you provide sensible solutions that create WOW you'll be regarded as indispensable. So allow your questions to be hypothetical, open, reflective, and even ridiculous and provocative. The reason you prepare diligently is so that you can make it easy for today's customer to understand and appreciate your value. Your plan is to get inside their mind and their issues, so you can provide a solution for their unique challenges.

Belief Warning

When you prepare, be careful that you don't take all information at face value. Albert Einstein said, "Not everything that counts can be counted; not everything that can be counted counts." The following are some points to consider when you gather and assess information to create the perfect solution for today's customer.

- ☐ Are they the right customer for you? Even Lady Gaga would struggle to sell concert tickets to fans of AC/DC. Remember this; make it customised and comprehensive for the correct customer.

- ☐ A surge in sales may not represent a developing trend. It could be a seasonal success.

- ☐ You may need information outside today's customer's industry if you want to anticipate their needs.

- ☐ Order efficiency may have satisfied today's customer last year, but their needs may have changed.

- ☐ Are you collecting and analysing too much information or incorrect information?

- Do you possess enough information to give your information true meaning?

- Most information is always out of date. How out of date is yours?

- How many touching points will you need to make a sale?

- How many influencers will you need to unite behind an agreement?

Kelly's Customer Compass ™

Let's look at how you can increase your odds of success in a B2B (business to business) environment. Please note that many of these observations apply to a B2C (business to consumer) environment also. *Kelly's Customer Compass* ™ will help you do your homework. This authentic analysis will support you in your bid to become a potential partner and a trusted supplier. This will support the conversation you enjoy with today's customer online, by phone, or face-to-face.

Ask yourself these questions.

1. Is today's customer a cold prospect, a warm lead, a hot prospect, a qualified new customer, a golden customer, or a glowing evangelist?

2. Where is today's customer based and why? Are they segmented into psychographic, geographic, and demographic, behavioural profiles?

3. What are today's customer's needs and wants? You can Google them, follow them on Twitter, read industry publications, call their PR department, analyse your CRM information, or you can seek a connection on LinkedIn or other social media.

4. Who else can advise me and support me with relevant information?

5. Who else does today's customer buy from?

6. In a world of conscious consumption, can I prove that my company's, products and services serve the world on a moral level too?

7. Where do I think I can add value by solving a problem or offering a breakthrough?

8. Do I need to sell the market's position before I communicate value?

9. Will I be communicating with the decision maker?

10. Does today's customer know my other customers?

11. What are the three biggest results today's customer can expect from dealing with me?

12. Can I meet a financial leader of a company and emphatically explain a return on investment? Can I communicate in terms of market share, return on sales and equity, retention of a customer base, and revenues saved and earned? Do I have suggested criteria for how to measure future success?

Can I quantify the benefit ("Our service saves you 56 hours on overtime and offers you a 23% increase in sales")?

13. Do I have proof of where my products and services improved a company's reputation, morale, customer service, etc.?

14. What separates me from my current and possible competitors – brand value; point of sale promotions etc.?

15. Do I know my competitors' prices?

16. What's my competitors' latest product or service launch?

17. What's the industry perspective on what I offer?

18. How has today's customer's company evolved?

19. Has the company received positive or negative media coverage recently?

20. Does my company have price rises on the way?

21. Will my competitors raise their prices soon?

22. Are my products and services exclusive?

23. Am I offering a limited time only offer?

24. Who'll like my products and services the most?

25. Why am I the best person to deal with?

26. What are today's customer's true buying motives?

27. Do I know today's customer's industry jargon? Am I prepared to use it in my communication?

28. What are my company's brand values and how do they match today's customer's brand values?

29. Have I interacted with my marketing team recently? Have I integrated my company's advertising, sales promotions, promotional education, and other branding into my preparation?

30. What are my company's retention rates, complaints, and satisfaction rates? Is there an up to date statistic that will support my communication?

31. How long will the sales process take?

32. What's the most important thing for today's customer?

33. What's my competition's biggest weakness in the mind of today's customer?

34. Can I reveal what people who refused my proposal bought from me as an alternative?

35. Is my evidence supported by an independent or reliable expert?

36. Am I as excited about my products and services as I should be, or have I become complacent?

37. Am I selling a cure or prevention? Can I express myself in a way that supports either?

38. Have I developed a plan that will sell benefits and solutions over features?

39. Is my evidence consistent with today's customer's values?

40. Are my statistics real and authentically described? You can describe a profit margin drop from 20 to 10 per cent as a drop of 10 percentage points. You can also describe it as a drop of 50 per cent. Make sure today's customer understands the truth.

41. Is any of my historical information still true today?

42. What guarantee extensions can I offer?

43. What are the cultural sensitivities I must avoid and how will I avoid them?

44. What are the possible opportunities to upsell and cross sell?

45. What are the possible opportunities for sequential selling?

46. What can I help today's customer with if they don't buy this time?

47. How many other quotes may today's customer get?

48. Do I have high value complementary packages I can offer if there's an opportunity to upsell?

49. Why did today's customer not buy the last time my company offered them products and services?

50. What's the number-one thing that can stop today's customer making a decision?

Please do your homework and create an evidence based emotional picture. There's no room for hypothetical facts and figures, or promises you can't keep. You must only give intelligently and ethically sourced correct information if you truly want to sell with WOW. Use *Kelly's Customer Compass* ™ to discover the information that will help you create a positive transformation for today's customer.

Winners reduce guesswork through investigation, so their conversations are devoid of waffle. They accept that an evidence based emotional picture requires a deep understanding of the tangible and intangible benefits of every offer. You can't maintain a conversational and non-pressured sales approach if you don't prepare to show you care.

> "Every time today's customer meets you, you're the brand.
> You build or destroy it
> at every touching point."
>
> **Darren Kelly**

The Super Confident 30-Second Pitch

After you distil your information for the solution you offer, can you please rehearse a 30-Second pitch? A 30-second pitch will usually consist of 75 words. You must be able to give a passionate and concise 30-second pitch of your value. You must also be able to reduce your pitch to a 140 character Twitter message. Now, let's go one stage further. Can you reduce it to a newspaper headline? This is important because more people read the headline than the story. Not only will you be able to discuss your offer in 30 seconds; your essential information will provide a launch pad for your meeting.

Remember that your 30-Second pitch can be your advertisement to start a profitable relationship with today's customer. You must give it the essence of WOW. Your message must have clarity, and it must have today's customer's interests in mind. This is how you create your message.

- Begin with a question that causes reflection about a current event or future challenge.

- Reveal exactly what it is you do. Describe this with a benefit for today's customer.

- Reveal what solution you offer today's customer.

- Reveal what differentiates you from your competition.

- Reveal why today's customer should listen beyond 30 seconds.

You might need your pitch at a trade show, on the phone, at an event, or while you're stuck in a lift. Here's an example. "Bill. Have you ever had the opportunity to spend a day with your sales team on the job? I help sales teams recover missed opportunities to drive revenue above target. My training is totally focused on your specific issue of reaching and persuading today's customer. Would you like to see how I've helped my customer base increase their sales on average 23% over the past two years?"

I never said that being a great salesperson is easy, but when you combine your inner confidence with the confidence of knowing you're prepared you'll be unstoppable. You'll offer the honesty and sincerity to build relationships, and the confidence to maintain today's customer's trust.

You'll feel better if you consider yourself a salesperson with strategic value as opposed to a self-serving salesperson. When you communicate in a way that suggests a sophisticated understanding of today's customer's business priorities you'll torpedo your competition with WOW.

The 5% Principle

This is one of the shortest paragraphs in the book. It's short because life can throw you a curve ball at any moment. Things happen that you would never expect. Today's customer can die, a colleague may let you down, your partner may get sick, your products may be damaged, or your car may break down. If you live with WOW self-belief and values, you'll always find the support you need for these moments.

HELLO PROFIT Challenge 7

Meeting Bill

Imagine you're offered a face-to-face meeting with Bill Gates. Your goal is to sell him a piece of software that will reduce costs for The Bill and Melinda Gates Foundation. You've only one chance to convince him of your product's value. Think about how you would feel sitting with Gates. Would you be excited, scared, nervous, or perhaps worried? Spend five minutes thinking about this scenario. Please don't read any further until you do this.

Meeting Bill again

How would you feel and what you would say if you were 10 times more confident meeting Bill Gates? Please remember that I'm referring to confidence and not arrogance. Think about how you would walk, speak, and listen. Would you walk faster, speak more clearly, and listen more patiently? What would you wear, and how would Bill Gates respond? Would you wear what's respectful and comfortable, or would you dress like someone you're not? Would Bill Gates listen respectfully and enjoy the conversation, or would he look bored? Spend five minutes thinking about this scenario. Please don't read any further until you do this.

10TY (10 Times You)

The picture you create in your mind before the meeting will dictate the outcome of the meeting. Your ability to undersell yourself can be your biggest enemy. What's the difference between your first meeting with Bill and your second meeting after discovering your 10TY (10 Times You) confident self? Reassess what you've done, and what you can offer to take you closer to your 10TY confident self. If you still find the idea of being 10TY strange, think about the minus 10TY that you may have created in the past. The minus 10TY is an average salesperson who lists every reason why they shouldn't succeed. Don't create an image that becomes your biggest enemy. Create an image that empowers you to communicate the incredible value you offer, so today's customer thinks **WOW**.

8. Rapport for Relationships

"Rapport is the number one skill of communication."

Darren Kelly

- ☐ Superstar WOW
- ☐ WOW-Mart
- ☐ Eyes of WOW
- ☐ Remember My Name
- ☐ Rapport in Ruins
- ☐ Rapport Can't Lie
    1. The Big Fat Lie
    2. The Reckless Lie
    3. The Inner Lie
    4. The Silent Lie
- ☐ The Lie Detector
- ☐ Rapport to Remember
- ☐ Rapport in Meetings
- ☐ QEA - Questions, Empathy, Answers

☐ Rapport with Groups

☐ Rapport from Refusals

☐ Rapport after Sales

☐ **HELLO PROFIT Challenge 8**

   The number one reason your proposal failed
   Wait! Your proposal may not have failed

Superstar WOW

You can't sell with WOW unless you can show today's customer that you're on their side. Think of rapport as good feelings shared between two or more persons. It's built on genuine respect, understanding, and empathy. Rapport is the foundation for every agreement and relationship. If you can't establish rapport with today's customer offline and online, you might as well bin your products, or cancel your services. Why? Because persuasion before rapport is never going to happen: you must be in synch with today's customer if you wish to persuade them. They want to feel that you think on their wavelength and that you care.

Rapport can only be achieved if you stop thinking about yourself, and demonstrate that you understand and respect today's customer's thoughts and feelings. In 2005, I interviewed the biggest male Latino singer in the world - Ricky Martin. The interview at Heart FM was scheduled for 4pm. I waited for him in my radio studio for 30 minutes before I questioned whether he was going to arrive or not. As I left my studio I noticed a large crowd outside the radio station. Among the screaming fans was a man scribbling on paper, t-shirts, books, and CD's. It was Martin working his way through the 200 plus fans who had come to catch a glimpse of him. He could've easily offered them a wave and passed them by, but he cared too much to do that. When we met we shook hands, and I gave him my congratulations for his work with The Ricky Martin Foundation. It was genuine respect because I'd run The London Marathon to raise money for vulnerable children in Britain, and I admired Martin's charitable work. His face lit up, and he thanked me for appreciating his work. Martin proved to be the perfect example of a star who delivered WOW. He may have been selling records all over the world, but his love for his fans and his desire to contribute to a better world meant more to him than his personal success. When you possess that attitude of service, and you back it up with a hard earned skillset you'll build rapport with most people you meet.

Here's another example of superstar WOW from Cher, a singer and actress who won an Oscar, a Grammy, an Emmy, and a Golden Globe. She also sold over 100 million albums. I interviewed her for *The Farewell Tour*, and she amazed me away within the first five minutes. As you can imagine, I prepared for the interview, but I didn't expect her to interview me, and to show she cared about my life. She asked me questions about my hometown Dublin, my wife, the TV comedy *Father Ted*, my career, and life as a radio personality. That was an example of superstar WOW – putting the other person first. How do you think I felt and sounded when I promoted her songs and the tour? Building rapport isn't about a slick technique. It truly comes from the heart before the head. I know you care for today's customer because you're reading this book. My aim in this chapter is to help you communicate the fact that you care.

WOW-Mart

One of the biggest companies in the world was founded by a man who understood the value of rapport. Sam Walton was born on 29 March, 1918 in Kingfisher, Oklahoma. 80 years later, he appeared in *Time's* list of the 100 Most Influential People of the 20th Century. *Forbes* magazine ranked him as the richest man in the USA, from 1982 to 1988. How did a young boy who milked cows and sold newspapers grow up to build a shopping giant that would operate in the USA, Canada, South America, China and the UK? His Wal-Mart stores, which now own ASDA UK, were built on astute team building, and a desire to offer its customer base the lowest prices possible. To achieve this, Walton knew he couldn't rely solely on his BA in Economics. He understood he'd have to motivate, inspire, and lead his employees, and engage with every customer on a level no other retailer could've ever comprehended at the time.

Walton was a child of The Great Depression, and his people skills were moulded by his mother. She suggested to the young boy that he should greet people enthusiastically when he met them. She also advised him to say their names first, and to reach out and shake their hands. This advice served him well as a trainee manager at a JC Penney store, and later as an American Army Captain during World War II. These skills of rapport also helped him create success as a Ben Franklin store franchisee, and later at Wal-Mart. During his time working at JC Penney, a member of the personnel team told Walton he only kept his job because of his sales skills. He was so engrossed with his customer base that, in the early years, he was weak in the clerical aspects of the job.

Walton's story shows us how his absolute respect for his customer base helped make him the world's richest man. His philosophy was more about saving his customer money than taking their money. Because he cared and got the first bit right, the second part happened more easily. These skills were also used to motivate his employees at Wal-Mart. He later summed up his business philosophy when he accepted the *Gold Medal Award* from the National Retail Merchants Association in 1988. He said Wal-Mart believed in people and in developing partnerships. He maintained communication excellence by never allowing his failures or setbacks to change his thoughts on the value of people.

Eyes of WOW

Walton lost a successful Ben Franklin franchise store in 1950 in Newport, Arkansas because his landlord wanted his own son to have the store. He was devastated because he'd worked so hard to make it the busiest store in the region, but he'd failed to read the lease properly when he signed it. Walton, his wife Helen and their young family moved to Bentonville, Arkansas, and he developed a chain of other Ben Franklin franchises until he founded Wal-Mart in Rogers, Arkansas in 1962. All the other retailers thought he was foolish to build shopping centres away from the big towns that had higher incomes. However, Walton's plan was backed up by his extensive face-to-face customer intelligence. He was known to stand outside his competitors stores for hours. He'd ask every customer what they desired, so they'd shop in his store one day.

When 74-year-old Walton died in 1992, the New York Times called him, "the most successful merchant of his time." He was honoured by President George Bush senior with the *Presidential Medal of Freedom*, the highest honour an American citizen can receive. Walton will also be remembered for his ability to have fun with his customer base, and how he used those skills to build an empire. You must build rapport with today's customer like Walton did. You may be selling products and services, but from today's customer's perspective, they're buying something to feel better.

> "Friendship is a single soul dwelling in two bodies."
>
> **Aristotle**

Remember My Name

Let's look at Walton's mother's advice about the importance of a person's name. Why is it that some salespeople use the word "mate" when speaking to today's customer? Is it laziness? Is it habit? Is it carelessness? Is it fear of intimacy? Is it because they never bother to listen as carefully as Walton did? Other words used are "bud, bro, son, girl, lad, lass, and luv." If you say these words in a friendly way, have you ever wondered that the person hearing them may think you're too lazy to remember their name? For most people, their name is a symbol of love, which started when they were a baby. Their parents and family called them that name and mixed it up with other childhood affections. Their name is embedded with trust and loyalty and unconditional love. It's the name their best friends called them at school, and the name that was written on every birthday card they ever received. When they hear it, the emotional connection creates WOW. Think about the power of Coke's *Share a Coke* campaign.

A great salesperson makes a point of remembering today's customer's name. Some will write the name as soon as possible, or others will ask the person to repeat it, or ask a question about it. "Is that Zach with a CH or a K?" This skill of respecting people's names helped Walton come to the attention of *Forbes* magazine who valued his wealth at $2.8 billion in 1985. He made a point of remembering people's names and using their names whenever he greeted them. Is it any wonder Walton was known for his sincerity and deep understanding of human emotion?

Another issue you may encounter is the pronunciation of names. Have you met a customer whose name was unfamiliar to you, and you were unable to say it correctly? Try the following. "I like your name. Can you help me pronounce it properly?" Which scenario makes you look better; you saying their name in error for the next ten meetings, or you showing them respect from the start? This also has the added benefit of reducing your stress level. Now every time you meet today's customer you're not thinking, "Oh dear. How do you pronounce his or her name?" If you don't believe the importance of this, list the five most important people in your life. When you write their names think about how seeing and saying their names makes you feel. If mentioning their names has an emotional impact on you, how do you think they feel about their own name? Asking a person about their name puts you into a position where you must listen, and this reinforces rapport.

Rapport in Ruins

One way to break rapport with today's customer is to withhold the truth, or to tell a blatant lie. We're all born liars. We've all told a lie, and if you tell me that you've never told a lie from birth to now, I may suggest you're lying. People also lie about their lies by grading them. They'll justify their lie as being a white lie. I'm not saying that we're all Charles Ponzi or Bernie Madoff clones, but let's look at the logic here. As a baby, you'll have faked a cry to get your parents attention at some stage. As a teenager, you'll have told your parents lies about where you went after school, or a lie that would spare their feelings. As an adult, you'll have lied to spare someone's feelings although that was probably not your real motive.

When people refuse to tell someone the truth it's usually to spare their own feelings from a possible backlash. This happens in many companies. I heard about one prominent leader who asked his employees if they were overstretched after a series of cutbacks. No one put their hand up because they feared their card would be marked. That sort of dishonesty destroys a business. I blame the leader because he trained his employees to lie to him. He did this by only promoting people who agreed with him.

Here's a terrific way to discover if someone is telling you a lie. Listen to the order of their story. They'll most likely tell it in chronological order so they'll remember it. If you question them by taking their story backwards, it will be harder for them to remember their lie.

When today's customer is blatantly lied to, the relationship becomes like a mended piece of china. You'll always know there's a repaired crack, and it will lose its value. The stress point is a reminder of the overall weakness. One instance of intentional deceit will ruin the relationship forever. You may recover and continue to work with today's customer, but you'll lose their loyalty, and they'll question everything you say forever. Too many salespeople make deceitful promises and under deliver. This is such a short term strategy and very much misguided. Apart from questioning their ethics you must wonder how long they'll be in business.

Jack Welch was dubbed *Manager of the Century* by *Fortune* magazine in 1999. He was chairman of General Electric from 1981 until he retired in 2001. In 1997, the company recorded a $200 billion capitalisation. No other company in the world had yet achieved this goal. Welch's motto was that you should be straight and tell people the truth. He said people knew the truth anyway, or they'd find out soon enough, and you only lose credibility with a lie.

> *"I'm not upset that you lied to me,*
> *I'm upset that from now on*
> *I can't believe you."*
>
> **Friedrich Nietzsche**

Rapport Can't Lie

There's a myth that says America's first president George Washington confessed to chopping down a cherry tree when he was a boy. The myth says that Washington came clean because in his own words, "I cannot tell a lie." However, the same George Washington was also renowned for leading people to believe he was more energetic than they thought. When Washington travelled from town to town during the American War of Independence, he would descend from his carriage before entering every town. A refreshed Washington would mount his white horse Nelson, and ride valiantly into town. Was he hiding an untruth, or was he just engaged in 18th Century Marketing? If Washington had been caught out, his image wouldn't have been tarnished significantly. However, in today's world of social media, Washington would've been lampooned on every website that cared. The great deterrent for leaders and salespeople who lie today is that the lie will always come back, and the bite on the bum will be extremely painful.

A statement of error either deliberately or recklessly delivered will harm your character. Because character is a greater attribute than personality in building and maintaining trust, you'll lose more than you'll ever know. However, as silence is also a form of misrepresentation, what you don't say may also help you lose your credibility. Today's customer places all misrepresentations under the banner called a lie. Can a salesperson recover from telling a lie? History shows us that people are more willing to forgive a lie if it doesn't impact them directly. However, if it does impact them directly, it's almost impossible for the liar to regain their trust. There are four main lies that weaken a salesperson's character - The Big Fat Lie, The Reckless Lie, The Inner Lie, and The Silent Lie.

1. The Big Fat Lie

The Wizard of Oz, Lance Armstrong, and Bernie Madoff take some beating when it comes to lying, but let's look at a big one that killed a president's career. On 17 November, 1973, America's 37th president, Richard Nixon, infamously dismissed any possible involvement in the Watergate scandal. Two reporters, Bob Woodward and Carl Bernstein discovered that a break-in at the Democratic headquarters in the Watergate hotel was linked to the Nixon administration. The crucial question was - Did Nixon know about it? Nixon told the people of America, "I am not a crook." Recorded White House conversations told a different story, and Nixon resigned before he could be impeached.

2. The Reckless Lie

Even an honestly felt but inaccurate statement can be perceived as being a lie. America's 31st president, Herbert Hoover made such an error on 25 October, 1929. Hoover said the following words only four days before the Stock Market collapsed. "The fundamental business of the country, that is, production and distribution of commodities, is on a sound and prosperous basis."

In 1988, George Bush senior made his most famous statement, "Read my lips. No new taxes." The slogan propelled Bush into the White House as America's 41st president. Bush reluctantly raised taxes later, but his broken promise handed Bill Clinton a weapon to help defeat him in the 1992 election.

3. The Inner Lie

Sometimes the most horrific lies we tell are the ones we tell ourselves. If we lie to ourselves, we blind ourselves to many dangers. John F. Kennedy lied to himself over *The Bay of Pigs* failure. Kennedy was a victim of arrogance and self-preservation. Before the presidential election in 1960, he'd accused America's 34th president, Dwight Eisenhower of being soft on Cuba, a country only 90 miles away from America's shores. Kennedy placed himself in a position where if he'd backed down, the Republican Party would've branded him weak. Kennedy later admitted his error in judgement, and for this, he was rightly applauded. He reflected on the fact that he took the wrong advice because the advice at the time suited his ego.

4. The Silent Lie

John F. Kennedy delivered a speech to the Massachusetts state legislature before he became president. Kennedy said that his presidency would be judged by "the high court of history." He mentioned courage, judgment, integrity, and dedication as being the criteria for such judgement. There's much debate over Kennedy's legacy. He inspired America to go to the moon, he fought for racial equality, and he showed profound honesty when he took responsibility for *The Bay Of Pigs* failure. However, much has been written about Kennedy laying down the country's moral law while indulging in behaviour more suitable to a rock star. Is it possible for a leader or salesperson to separate their public and personal integrity? Can a person say, "I lie to all my family, but you can trust me in politics and business"?

The Lie Detector

When pilots board a plane they know they must assume full responsibility for the safety of their passengers. This forces them to study the plane and sign off their safety checklist before departure. The same is true for when you communicate. You're responsible for checking the legitimacy of all your facts. Comment is free, but facts are extremely sacred. Today's customer may not accept your apology if your outdated or incorrect information delivers an untruth that harms them. It's you who must take the blame for any errors. When you decide to enter a fact in any conversation, speech, or presentation, it's wise to check your facts from two verified sources and ask yourself the following questions.

☐ Who said so?

☐ What are their qualifications to say so?

☐ Who agrees with them?

☐ What are the qualifications of those who agree?

☐ Do the facts represent new information?

☐ How do the facts differ from previous information?

☐ What do other experts say?

☐ Have any of the experts been found to have lied about anything before?

☐ In what way do the experts benefit from offering their facts? Are they impartial?

☐ Does today's customer have information that contradicts any of my facts?

☐ Can I use a fact, but highlight that it can change at any moment?

Rapport to Remember

If you want today's customer to grasp your value and remember it, you must employ repetition skilfully. It helps the retention of a moment of WOW. Repetition in Martin Luther King's, *I Have a Dream* speech helped move an audience of over 250,000 people. It's worth taking a closer look at repetition in King's speech. The word "freedom" was used 20 times. The word "justice" was used eight times, and "injustice" three times. The word "dream" was used 11 times. Would you agree that King's dream for freedom, justice, and unity was supported by his use of repetition?

Repetition is crucial. If you're speaking to persuade today's customer that a new product you have is easy to use, you might say, "It's easier than you think." However, an average salesperson falls into the trap of trying to say the same thing later on with different words. So instead of repeating, "It's easier than you think," they might say, "It's not as difficult as you think." Repetition acts as a reminder of key points, and it also glues the elements of a conversation, speech, or presentation together. You may think this is a minor point, but King didn't and great salespeople don't.

Rapport in Meetings

This is an example of how a great salesperson creates rapport in a sales meeting after a genuine greeting.

- They discover what today's customer's challenges are, and what's top of their mind. They ask genuine questions that show a genuine regard to care for their needs.

- They naturally pick up today's customer's preferred communication sense, whether that's sight, hearing, or feeling dominant. You may say that you do speak in the language today's customer speaks, and yes you do, but perhaps only 50 per cent of the time. Let me explain this further, so you can see, hear, or feel what I mean. Some people may say, "I see what you're saying," or "I hear you," or "You've touched me." These are different words, but they all mean the same thing. The first has a visual; the second has a sound, and the third has a feeling communication sense. Most people use a dominant sense in the language they use, and if you listen carefully, you'll be able to communicate using words that reflect that dominant sense, whether it's visual, sound, or feeling. The senses of taste and smell are not used as frequently as the other three senses in most conversations (except of course, when food is the topic). A great salesperson is a great communicator and can use all the senses equally if required. They know that when you need to help today's customer understand a point, it helps if you possess the ability to communicate in their preferred sense.

☐ They listen carefully to discover if today's customer speaks in detail, or if they offer a big picture. They also listen carefully to hear if today's customer thinks more in the past, present, or future.

☐ They naturally adopt today's customer's body language and subconsciously synch with them. When you have a genuine desire to help today's customer, and you find a common ground, you'll naturally match their breathing speed, and the pitch, volume, and speed of their speech. You'll also find yourself matching some of their body movements. If you look at or listen to two people who are in love, or who connect on a business basis, you'll see in both cases that their words and body language have more matches than mismatches. I'm not a fan of matching and mirroring today's customer's body language mechanically. I think such unnatural behaviour is immoral, but there's another reason too. What happens if today's customer discovers what you're doing, or if they're trying to do it to you? You'll both end up moving like two dysfunctional robots. My message is clear on this point. If you care, you don't have to mess about with trying to fake rapport.

☐   They adapt to any doubt or disagreement that's evident in today's customer's body language.

A great salesperson knows that continuous rapport is maintained by a feeling of trust. Without rapport, your intention to help today's customer may seem intrusive. Trust is always built from honestly putting today's customer's needs and wants first. However, you must communicate trust effectively, so today's customer understands that their interests are your top priority. This rule of rapport also applies to lawyers, marketing executives, accountants, leaders, PR executives and medical experts.

A surgeon can use their expertise and diligence to save a person's life against the odds, but they also know that their bedside manner with their patient must be excellent. A surgeon may have sacrificed a night out with their family, or worked extra hours to operate successfully, but they could lose their patient's respect, trust, and appreciation if they communicate ineffectively before and after the operation. It probably sounds harsh and illogical, but emotions more often than not will override logic. Your aim is to communicate with clarity and confidence, so you create a relationship of cooperation. Show you care and maintain your integrity.

> *"He who asks a question is a fool for five minutes; he who does not ask a question remains a fool forever."*
>
> **Chinese Proverb**

QEA - Questions, Empathy, Answers

The simplest way to think about rapport is QEA (Questions, Empathy, and Answers).

Questions

Questions are one of the keys to rapport, but an average salesperson feels they should be offering more answers than questions. They believe that today's customer feels uncomfortable when they're questioned. This isn't true because questions open today's customer's mind to beneficial things they may not have thought about. In the same way that a doctor would never diagnose an illness before asking a series of questions, you can never identify today's customer's true needs and wants without effective questions. Asking questions effectively and confidently requires skill and focus. Your job isn't to increase the size of their problem, but to show it for what it is, and how you can solve it. If you ask your questions insensitively, you may sound like an abrupt legal prosecutor. Remember the following.

- Never ask more than one question at a time. You'll only overburden today's customer.

- Never fail to start your questions with warm and engaging words that prove understanding and respect. "You said time is an issue. How much is that costing you?"

- Never start your conversation with questions that begin with "Are" and "Do" because they lead to closed-ended questions. Save them for after you've built rapport.

☐ Open ended questions propel the conversation while closed-ended questions are useful for ending the conversation or for requesting a decision.

☐ Never answer your own questions. You want a dialogue, not a self-obsessed monologue.

☐ Never resist the urge to remain silent. Force silence on yourself after you ask a question about an important issue.

☐ Never use intensifiers like "surely" and "very." They weaken your words.

☐ Seek permission to ask deeper questions to gather more information, or to help today's customer understand your solution. Their responses will help you zoom in on what's most important for them. Remember that the purpose of your preparation isn't to offer you a strict approach, but to allow you to be more agile to the demands of every interaction with today's customer. You must listen effectively because they may mention a problem that you may have a solution for.

Empathy

Think of a time you won a person over by seeing things their way. Isn't it true that the other person's attitude to you changed when you validated their opinion and appreciated the intensity of their emotions? Empathy is essential in any conversation, but please don't confuse this with being a "yes" person. You can empathise with today's customer's reasons for thinking a certain way, or empathise with their emotional intensity, even if they're wrong. Your empathy forms the bridge that allows your answers to be received and understood. Where there are differences in opinion and personality, you should always look to the areas of common agreement and personality first. This helps to cement rapport in any relationship. You should never disagree before you at least discover what you and today's customer agree on first.

Have you ever had the best interests of a family member or friend in mind and your logical solution seemed the right one? Did you feel bewildered because they either dismissed your words, or they accepted them, but they never took action? Did you perhaps jump too quickly with a solution before they were ready to accept it? Perhaps your advice was pure genius, but could it possibly have been an error in your communication skills that sabotaged the rapport, and shut the door of their mind? When logic isn't accepted and trusted, you may just find it's because rapport has been broken. If you want to discover if rapport exists during a meeting, just ask yourself if today's customer speaks more than you. Also ask if they include you as a possible solution to their challenge. If the answer to those questions is positive, you probably have rapport.

When you empathise remember

- not to use the word 'but.' Use the word 'and.' 'But' is confrontational and negates everything said before it.

- to never waste today's customer's objections. Use them to clarify things, or to pinpoint a genuine concern.

Answers

This is the part of a conversation where a great salesperson's preparation and character offers them the flexibility to create a *One-Win* solution. Instead of saying 'You win, and I win' you should ask 'How can we win together so our community benefits too?' That's how long-term relationships are developed and maintained.

Here's an example of how continuous rapport can be achieved and easily broken. Today's customer tells a salesperson that he thinks the salesperson's products are too difficult to operate, or his services are too expensive. A great salesperson will acknowledge today's customer's feelings first by saying something like, "I understand why you may think that. Everyone thinks differently about it after I explain how simple they are to use," or "how cheaper our services work out over a year." When you show appreciation for someone's feelings, you show them the utmost respect. An average salesperson will react with blunt dismissive replies like "No, they're really easy to use," or "They're cheaper than XYZ," or "They're not as expensive as you think." You must show respect before you dream of trying to change today's customer's opinion. This isn't a golden technique: it's just common sense. Your job isn't to be always right about your products and services, but to do right by today's customer.

☐ Never veer off your area off expertise and try to fake an answer.

☐ Never say "You'll have to speak to someone else," or "….that's not my department." Say "Let me find the person who can sort this problem out for you," or "I'll sort it out."

☐ Never use disclaimers to hide from any responsibility. Sentences such as "It's not my field, but I think…," lose you respect.

☐ Always be willing to suggest an alternative to your views and today's customer's views. The alternative can be a combination of the best ideas of both sides, and they may create the perfect example of *One-Win*.

☐ Use marketing materials and qualified data, and provide demonstrations when they're required to prove a point.

Rapport with Groups

This is tricky because you're dealing with different personalities who may have different agendas. You may face the ultimate decision maker, the financial director, the ultimate user, an adviser, and an observer masquerading as a minutes taker! Feedback is usually limited, and you can almost feel as if you're on trial. You can't focus on one person because while that person may seem to dominate the process, they may not have the power to make the ultimate decision. The best solution isn't to play games. Simply discover who you're speaking to and shape your message, so it facilitates the solving of their problems. Your responses to any questions will be judged more than your presentation. This means you can't respond disrespectfully to one person and expect your biggest fan not to think badly of you. So if one person treats you badly, simply smile and stay professional.

You must always assume that you're selling with WOW to a team, even if you only face one person. That's why you must respect everyone in a company: you never know which agent of influence can help you win or lose an agreement. This understanding is also necessary in a retail environment where a salesperson may have to communicate with one person, two partners, or a small group.

Rapport from Refusals

One of the most understated ways to build rapport is to turn down a sale. The temptation is to grab every agreement, but what if it's wrong for today's customer. Think about this. Have you ever bought an item of clothing and the salesperson recommended something else. Maybe that 'something else' was cheaper, but it suited you better. Please pause to reflect on that moment. How did you feel? Isn't it true that a moment of magic was created and it bonded your loyalty to that salesperson and that store? You must remember that rapport creates a relationship, but you can't have rapport without trust and respect.

Rapport after Sales

An average salesperson neglects this part of rapport maintenance. The best companies in the world use today's customer's departure as a moment to build a future relationship. They do this by simply saying, "Thank you," and giving today's customer a reason to stay connected. Apple is exceptionally adept at this. When I bought my iPad, the customer service agent suggested I should send him pictures of my next presentation. This showed that he paid attention to my number one reason for buying my iPad. The customer service agent's enthusiasm was so strong and genuine that I felt a connection with the store. It reminded me that we don't mind being sold to if we enjoy the experience, and if the products and services are what we need and enjoy.

HELLO PROFIT Challenge 8

The number one reason your proposal failed

I'm often asked about the number one reason why many B2B and B2C proposals fail to win any business. The answer is straightforward; there was never any agreement in the first place. The salesperson probably enjoyed a polite discussion with today's customer who probably said, "I'll think about it. Can you send me a proposal?" The salesperson probably spent two nights typing up a proposal before they sent it to the customer first class. They probably followed this up with phone calls and emails, but today's customer never responded. The truth is that the request for a proposal may have been a ploy to get rid of the salesperson. Perhaps, it wasn't, and the proposal was too complicated for today's customer to read.

Remember; your proposal isn't an additional exploration of today's customer's needs and wants. It should only ever be written confirmation of the issues you agreed. It doesn't have to be a Pulitzer Prize winning book. Keep it simple and don't assume that the bigger the company, the bigger the proposal must be. Only commit to preparing a proposal if there's an agreement on the problem, the methods for the solution, the measures of success, the value offered, and the investment required. What's the point in offering a proposal that stuns today's customer when they read the price or terms? If that's the reason for failure, it's your fault. Remember that today's customer rarely gets better to deal with if you mess up the first time around.

Try the following rapport test to see if you and today's customer connected with **WOW** during your meeting.

☐ Did they accept your follow up phone call?

☐ Did they return your follow up phone call?

☐ Did they ask to meet you again or did you ask?

☐ Did they book the follow up so far into the future that you knew it probably wouldn't happen?

☐ Did they ask you to keep in touch?

☐   Did they say "Leave it with me" which translates into "Leave me alone"?

The truth is that you connected with today's customer and you offered them irresistible value, or you didn't.

Wait! Your proposal may not have failed

Now what happens if you did everything I suggested above, but your prospective customer seems to be ignoring you. Here's some sound advice from the brilliant sales speaker and strategist Jill Konrath, the author of *Snap Selling*. She makes a powerful point about what to do when a glowing prospective customer fades away despite you offering your A game. The unreturned phone call or email can hurt a salesperson's confidence and make them think they've lost a customer. Konrath suggests that every salesperson must shift their mind-set to one of a persistent go-getter especially if a prospective customer has shown enthusiastic interest. She correctly points out that the prospective customer may be overwhelmed with urgent and demanding priorities.

Konrath uses a superb example to make her point. She speaks about going to the dentist. We all know it's vital for our health to care for our teeth, but many of us don't give it top priority. Thankfully most dentists send reminders – maybe a post card, text, or email. When some patients put the visit off they're reminded again, and they eventually make a decision to visit their dentist. But they may not have visited their dentist without the reminders. It's proof that today's customer must be reminded about your service with WOW.

Do you remind today's customer consistently about their priorities? Do your reminders express the importance of the irresistible value you offer? If you understand your prospective customer, and you believe in yourself and your products and services you'll adopt the dentist's approach because you care 100%. As Konrath rightly says, "It's okay to be a visible irritant. It actually helps your prospects."

9. Wisdom for Winning

*"Man's mind stretched by a new idea
never goes back
to its original dimensions."*

Oliver Wendell Holmes

- ☐ Forget Your Hot Air Balloon
- ☐ Find Your WOW Mentor
- ☐ Sound Wisdom
- ☐ Compulsory Learning
- ☐ Wisdom that Protects
- ☐ Mentor Mentee Guidelines
- ☐ SONY mentoring

- ☐ **HELLO PROFIT Challenge 9**

    You as a WOW Mentee
    You as a WOW Mentor

Forget Your Hot Air Balloon

You can't sell with WOW unless you possess wisdom. Wisdom is a deep understanding of knowledge and experience. You can gain wisdom from your own life and support it with a WOW mentor. This is my favourite definition of mentoring from an unknown author. "Mentoring is a process, in which a more skilled or more experienced person, serving as a role model, teaches, sponsors, encourages, counsels, and befriends a less skilled or less experienced person for the purpose of promoting the latter's professional and/or personal development. Mentoring functions are carried out within the context of an on-going, supportive relationship between the mentor and mentee."

A WOW mentor is essential because it's impossible to create an objective opinion of your work or strategies without one. The fact is that you're simply too close to see what's happening under your own nose. You're also too far away to see the limitless possibilities that the mind-set of another person may offer. That's why you need a reliable, respected, and honest viewpoint. I'm lucky to have WOW mentors. Donald Trump is one the greatest business mentors in the world. He said a mentor should offer a mentee challenges and opportunities. You can't argue with those words.

No salesperson is expected to know all the answers. However, a great salesperson knows where to find the answers. Carolyn McCall, the CEO who transformed the airline easyJet borrowed an idea from former TESCO CEO, Terry Leahy. Every TESCO leader under Leahy was encouraged to spend time on the frontline every year. McCall's top team are known to man easyJet's check in desks every year. Her desire to keep learning aligned with her clinical commercial acumen and strong communication skills is inspiring.

Your true power as a salesperson can be evaluated by the support system of specialised knowledge you've created. Doesn't it make sense to tap into the accumulated knowledge of the masters in your profession and beyond your profession? The difference between working solo and working with a WOW mentor or a WOW mastermind group is massive. It's similar to the difference between trying to fly to the moon in a hot air balloon and trying to fly there in a rocket.

Find Your WOW Mentor

I always say there are three kinds of WOW mentors. There are people who've excelled in the field of selling, people who've excelled in the field of sales training, and people who've had experiences outside selling that can transform your communication. You'll have had many WOW mentors in your life so far. Who helped you with the challenge of finding your first job or first car? Who pointed to the fact that you've got a special talent for something? Who do you admire and sometimes copy? Who helped you through the most difficult time in your life? This may be one person or a group, but every time you were supported, that was a mentor/mentee relationship. Your inspiration and support can come from anywhere, and any profession, so don't embrace mediocrity by blindly conforming to industry norms.

Another speedy route to mediocrity is to assume that a WOW mentor has to be older than you. I know of one 56-year old salesperson who mentored a 20-year old salesperson, who in return mentored him in the use of social media. Both salespeople increased their sales on average 27% in six months by helping each other. By offering you help, a WOW mentor returns the favour they received from the selling profession or another profession, and it makes them feel happy that a debt has been paid.

I'm often asked, "How do you find a WOW mentor if you can't find one in your own company, or in your business networks?" Find a person you admire: write them a letter, or call them to say why you respect their success. Ask them if they'd grant you 20 minutes of their time to help you progress in your career. Tell them you'll return the favour to someone who'll be learning the exciting art and science of selling one day.

Despite your request to receive help, you should treat the relationship as a two-way source of perspective and advice. This shows your WOW mentor that you're passionate, proactive, thoughtful, and worth spending time on. The world is full of takers, who live in a state of expectancy. A great salesperson isn't like that, and your approach to a WOW mentor must be the same. One nugget of information can transform your career, so ensure you take integrity and passion into this relationship.

*"Do not train a child to learn
by force or harshness;
but direct them to it
by what amuses their minds,
so that you may be better able
to discover with accuracy
the peculiar bent
of the genius of each."*

Plato

Sound Wisdom

Akio Morita was born on 26 January, 1921 in Nagoya, Japan. *Time* magazine named Morita as one of the 20 most influential business leaders of the 20th century. The company he co-founded has put its name on TV's, VCR's, DVD players, the Walkman, the PlayStation, mobile phones, eReaders, laptops, and more. The name Sony, which derives from a mix of the Latin word *sonus*, meaning sound, and the words *sonny boy*, is regarded as a mark of quality and style. Morita's story is certainly not a rags to riches tale. He was raised in a life of luxury, and his neighbours included the founders of the Toyota Company. As a young boy, Morita was destined to take over the family sake business, but his career choice changed after he graduated as a physicist from Osaka Imperial University in 1944. He joined the army as a physics researcher, and he made friends quickly with some of the most brilliant minds in Japan.

One of those friends was a colleague called Masaru Ibuka, who later became a co-founder of Sony. Morita's task in the army was to help Ibuka develop a heat-seeking bomb during World War II, and when the war ended in 1945 their friendship was united further by a business dream. On 7 May, 1946, a 25-year old Morita and a 38-year old Ibuka set up Tokyo Telecommunications Company, which later became Sony.

After a visit to America in 1952, Ibuka was convinced that the company's future lay in transistor radios. NBC had just started America's longest running TV show, *Today* and some people felt radio was on the way out. Morita and Ibuka thought differently, and the radios they created were a spectacular success. Perhaps, the seed for this electronic giant was sown years previous when a young Morita sat and listened to Bolero on his mother's electric phonograph. This was the moment Morita fell in love with sound. In 1958, the same year Tokyo Telecommunications Company became

Sony, it was Elvis who topped the charts, but today fans of Mariah Carey, One Direction, and others have lots of reasons to give thanks to these two men from Japan.

Compulsory Learning

The Sony Corporation of America was established in 1961, and Sony became the first Japanese company to be listed on the New York Stock Exchange. Morita was Sony's greatest salesperson during the early years. He examined every aspect of the sales process, even making his employees wear shirts with oversized pockets to support his claim that a particular Sony radio was pocket-sized. Morita communicated best practice with clarity, and he energised his salespeople further by sharing insights, formally and informally. Ibuka and Morita created a corporation that invited freedom and creativity, and they continually asked themselves, "How can we do things better?" Morita was responsible for Marketing, Finance, and Human Resources, and Ibuka looked after product development.

Both men sought new WOW mentors, like William Edwards Deming, an American consultant who taught business leaders in Japan how to improve aspects such as quality and sales. Deming said "Learning is not compulsory. . . neither is survival." He's also famous for saying, "It is not necessary to change. Survival is not mandatory." Two of the world's greatest salespeople who lavish praise on their mentors are Virgin boss Richard Branson and Warren Buffet. Branson found his WOW mentor in Freddie Laker, the founder of Laker Airlines when Virgin Airways was in its infancy. Buffet found his WOW mentor after he read the book *The Intelligent Investor*: it was the author, Benjamin Graham. In 2012, Buffet told *Forbes* magazine that from 1951 to 1954, he wrote to Graham to offer him securities ideas. His plan worked because Graham finally replied and he told Buffet to visit him in New York.

Wisdom that Protects

Morita's **WOW** mentor was a Hawaiian lawyer called Yoshinobo Kagawa. He advised Morita to start dressing like a businessman, and to live where businessmen lived. Morita accepted the fact that his scruffy clothing was sending out the wrong message to people he needed to influence. Morita was an exceptionally charming man who loved life, but he possessed inner steel that allowed him to face a truth when he was offered it. This insatiable desire for knowledge helped produce his success more quickly than even he expected. A great salesperson discovers a **WOW** mentor as early as possible in their career, and they continue to find **WOW** mentors until they retire. They know they can learn from an expert who has made the mistakes they don't need to make. They know that they can save themselves years of trial and error by adopting the hard earned lessons of others.

Morita was also a **WOW** mentor because he was an open source of knowledge on many subjects. He patiently explained how Sony worked and he advised his employees on how they could overcome setbacks and failures. He also shared his **WOW** values and his wisdom on how to embrace change. His integrity encouraged his employees to seek his confidential support and to have fun in their work. Every **WOW** mentor/mentee relationship that succeeds has an unwritten confidentiality clause. After all, no one wants to divulge their biggest weaknesses to the village gossip.

> *"Tell me and I forget,*
> *teach me and I may remember,*
> *involve me and I learn."*
>
> **Benjamin Franklin**

Mentor Mentee Guidelines

You as a mentee must think carefully about any constructive criticisms you receive before you respond to them. The truth can sting, even if it does you good. Morita once created an impressive tape recorder that was loved by many people, but no one would buy it. The reason was that it cost an average year's salary in Japan. Morita accepted that while he understood supply, he hadn't quite figured out the demand and affordability requirements for business. He changed his customer focus after he received some wise words from a colleague, and the tape recorder eventually sold.

Morita was responsible for mentoring many Japanese people as they integrated into American culture. He was also rewarded for his wisdom when he became the face of American Express. Morita loved working with younger people because they energised him with their enthusiasm and new ideas. The mentor/mentee relationship has benefits for both parties if you meet the right person or persons. When Morita died in 1999, former Sony Chairman, Norio Ohga recalled meeting Morita when Ohga was a university student in Japan in 1951. Morita spent time with Ohga and offered him some memorable words of encouragement.

Perhaps Morita's greatest lesson for business today was his assertion that a company isn't a commodity. He said a company is "just like a family." He also went as far to say that a company's short-term interests that create employee pain is a violation of human rights. This was a man who knew his WOW values: he defended Japan against an American backlash after Columbia Pictures was bought by Sony. Morita's responses were perfect examples of how you can lead people to the truth without upsetting them. He explained that many other American symbols had been purchased by other international companies. Morita's WOW mentors taught him well, and this compelled him to be true to himself. That's the type of salesperson and leader every company needs today. Your WOW mentor can offer you similar advice and support to help you sell with WOW.

> *"Do you want job security?*
> *Learn something valuable every day.*
> *Self-investment offers the best and*
> *most secure interest rates."*
>
> **Darren Kelly**

SONY mentoring

Morita's brilliant books *Gakureki Muyō Ron*, or *Never Mind School Records,* and *Made in Japan* reveal major insights for mentoring top talent in any company.

- ☐ School results should never be used to evaluate your competence after you get hired. You should be judged on your performance. Too many salespeople rely on training they did 20 years ago.

- ☐ Observe your mistakes. If you pretend you never made a mistake, or if you hide them you're bound to repeat them. Failure is one of the most important ingredients for success. Morita said you should never be afraid to make a mistake. But he also said it was silly to make the same mistake twice.

- ☐ Name a target to unleash your creativity. Even Michelangelo's Sistine Chapel masterpiece was guided by the Pope. Michelangelo was given a target, and it inspired his genius and dedication to success. Give yourself unique challenges that stretch you and inspire your creativity.

☐ Youthful input requires an honest and ego free environment. Leaders and mentors should welcome radical and innovative suggestions and criticisms from passionate employees. Morita hired Norio Ohga after he criticised Sony in a letter: Ohga would later become a Sony Chairman. Ohga was the man behind the CD (Compact Disc). The disc is 5 inches in diameter for a reason; it provides 75 minutes to store all of Beethoven's Ninth Symphony. Ohga was a big Beethoven fan! Ohga's CD led to the DVD and the CD-Rom. He also played a major part in the development of the PlayStation. Can you imagine if Morita had reacted differently when he received Ohga's letter of complaint? The letter criticised Sony for the terrible sound from its tape recorders. But Morita suppressed his ego, accepted the truth, and mentored a rising star. How many leaders would take the effort to do that?

When Sony released products in Morita's time there was less competition and people were slower to upgrade their products. We now live in a world where a product is updated every few months. Sony's rival Samsung adapted to this phenomenon of life affirming upgrades.

However, 2013 was a great year for Sony. The PS4 sold a million units within the first 24 hours of its release. Sony Pictures Television has enjoyed success over the last five years. It introduced us to a chemistry teacher called Walter White; a man who left his normal life for the underworld. The show made people think, 'What would I do if I was Walter?' *Breaking Bad* has been a TV sensation. I get the feeling that Sony is encouraging the kind of radical breakthroughs that Morita once encouraged. It would take a brave person to rule out Sony's return to the top of the entertainment world one day.

HELLO PROFIT Challenge 9

You as a WOW Mentee

When you meet your WOW mentor, consider the following questions.

- ☐ Who was their WOW mentor? This question reinforces the debt of gratitude they may feel they owe the sales profession.

- ☐ What was their attitude as a WOW mentee and what do they expect from one now? This helps you understand them and helps you see if your values, goals, and expectations connect.

- ☐ If you were eager to display the same courage, passion, dedication, and beliefs that they hold, would they be willing to help you?

- ☐ What time can they commit to for the WOW mentor/mentee relationship?

- ☐ When can you start working together?

- ☐ How can you add value to their career?

- ☐ Can you create a mastermind group?

- ☐ What are the rules for confidentiality?

- ☐ Where will you meet?

You as a WOW Mentor

Amazing things happen when you become a WOW mentor. Apart from the sheer happiness of helping another person, you'll discover many things about yourself. You'll also start to reinforce the lessons you may have forgotten. I get asked about how you know if you're ready to become a WOW mentor. There are a few things to think about, but I believe that these are the most important.

- ☐ Do you have experience and expertise in sales, customer service, or marketing?

- ☐ Do you have the time?

- ☐ Do you communicate well?

- ☐ Do you want to give back?

- ☐ Do you relate to different personalities?

- ☐ Do you possess a patient mind and an understanding heart?

- ☐ Do you have challenges and opportunities you can offer a mentee?

10. Passion for Promotion

"Nothing great in the world has ever been accomplished without passion."

Georg Hegel

- ☐ Passion by Design
- ☐ Connect the World
- ☐ Sleepy and Dopey
- ☐ WOW - An Apple Presentation

   1. The Ultimate Headline

   2. The Evil Enemy

   3. The Eloquence of Easy

   4. The Simple Solution

   5. The Exciting Feeling

   6. The Glorious Vision

7. The Everlasting Story

8. The Power of Punchy

9. The Gorgeous Goodbye

10. The Insanity of WOW

- [ ] When Things go Wrong
- [ ] The Laughing Matter
- [ ] The First Lady of WOW

- [ ] **HELLO PROFIT Challenge 10**

    Reignite Your Passion

Passion by Design

You can't sell with WOW in a speech or presentation unless you have passion. Passion is a strong and exciting feeling for someone or something. Have you ever spent time with a salesperson who loves their subject, products, or services? Isn't it true that their conviction oozed from every pore in their body? They didn't just promote their offer with words of reason, but with a force that swept you off your feet. Many people mistakenly believe that all passionate salespeople have passion naturally. In some cases, it's true, but in the majority of cases you'll find that these people made a decision to be passionate about their careers and their lives. Some people may say they're obsessed, as if that's a negative. What's wrong with wanting to do your best for your company and today's customer? Wouldn't you rather be filled with pride, knowing that your products, services, and communication created something special in today's customer's life?

In October 2011, we lost an example of a great salesperson who was passionate about design, but who also designed his own passion. Apple co-founder, Steve Jobs didn't see design as just the cover of a product: he saw design as the soul and every physical aspect of a product; inside and out. He didn't see selling as the delivery of information: he saw it as an enticing and enchanting life transforming visual feast.

Connect the World

Jobs was born on 24 February, 1955 in Los Altos, California. His biological mother was a young college graduate who put him up for adoption, but she insisted that his new parents send Jobs to college one day. Paul and Clara Jobs promised to increase their working class savings to fulfil that promise, but Jobs lost interest in college, and he left before he could graduate. No degrees catered for his computer dreams, so he decided to follow his heart and devote his life to a work that created WOW. His successes include co-founding Apple, the company that created the Mac, the iPod, the iPhone, the iPad, and iCloud.

In 1977, Jobs and his friend Steve Wozniak achieved enormous success when they sold the Apple II series. It was the first personal computer that most people could afford. The company, which started in Jobs garage, grew into a $2 billion company with 4,000 employees after only ten years. Apple was named after Jobs visited an apple farm. He was drawn to the wholesome image of the fruit. The logo is a play on the computer word byte. Jobs lost a power struggle with the Apple board of directors in 1985, and he was fired soon after. Isn't it staggering to think that a person can get fired from the company he co-founded? Walter Isaacson's brilliant book *Steve Jobs* highlights the Apple leader's tantrums and torment before and after that period. I prefer to concentrate on the skills and strategies that can propel your ability to sell with WOW.

After Apple (part 1) Jobs set up a computer company called NeXT, and he co-founded Pixar Animation Studios, which gave us *Toy Story*, and *A Bugs Life*. Apple's subsequent buyout of NeXT in 1996 returned Jobs to the company he helped to establish, and he served as its CEO until 2011. In that same year, Apple announced that it held the details of more than 225 million credit card accounts. No other online business in the world in 2011 had as many personal details to allow its customer base to buy with such ease.

Jobs created mass appeal for Apple through his understanding of the need to combine communication, entertainment, function, and elegance: this is how Apple connected the world. Jobs was a solutions minded person. He asked many probing questions, and he made sure he saw things in a positive and profitable light. He didn't seek 10% improvements. He looked for 100% improvements that made Apple stand alone in their field. The iPod and iPad are fashionable solutions to the problem of storing an entertainment and educational collection, and they allow instant access to all of it. The iTunes Store offers a solution for people's dislike of waiting for long periods to receive music, books, audio books, and movies from high street retailers.

> *"People will sit up and take notice of you if you will sit up and take notice of what makes them sit up and take notice."*
>
> **Harry Selfridge**

Sleepy and Dopey

When Jobs was at Pixar, he spoke about the influence of *Snow White and the Seven Dwarfs* on his career. He said it proved to him that technology comes and goes, but great stories are everlasting. This advice is essential: your challenge as a salesperson is to deliver a message that's enjoyed, understood, remembered, and acted upon. It's not an easy thing to do.

When you speak to an audience many people will listen to you with a caring attitude. They'll also listen with a desire to be educated and/or entertained. However, some people will listen selfishly by only paying attention to what concerns them. These people tune in and out when it suits them. You may also face critical or negative people who want to dismiss every word you say. They've got stored prejudices, experiences, and perhaps incorrect information that cause them to block all the information you deliver. Even in the face of logic and reason they're reluctant to open their minds to your words. So your challenge in your speech or presentation is to cut through the clutter in your audience's thoughts. You must do it

10. Passion for Promotion 189

in a way so that your words are understood, accepted, remembered, and acted upon.

All across the world, fortunes are squandered every year at conferences and product launches because salespeople fail to respect and prepare for their audiences. I believe that those salespeople who ramble with pointless, confusing, and bizarre speeches or presentations should face charges of attempted boredom. Self-obsessed salespeople who offer a series of facts with an overloaded PowerPoint screen should also face the same charges. You can't afford to deliver a speech or presentation without passionate precision. Too many bullet points and too much text torture your audience. If you make them feel sleepy they'll think you're dopey, and that's not good for business.

> "Dull PowerPoint makes presenting a doddle for a salesperson, but mind-numbing drudgery for today's audience."
>
> **Darren Kelly**

WOW – An Apple Presentation

Mark Twain said, "It usually takes me more than three weeks to prepare a good impromptu speech." Jobs always looked natural when he presented at Apple product launches because he prepared for several days. An average salesperson is either unskilled or wings it, but Jobs prepared to create WOW. This passion for promotion created a unique combination of authentic charisma and engaging polish.

Do you remember when he said an iPad was "more intimate than a laptop"? That wasn't an off the cuff remark, but perfectly placed words in his prepared presentation. When Jobs launched the iTunes store in 2003, he said "What that means is you'll......" You must always have those thoughts in your mind when you prepare a speech or presentation. What does your offer mean to your audience? You must offer value that serves your audience with WOW. You must also explain that value. When Jobs launched the iPod he said it had a 5GB hard drive. Ask five people what a 5GB hard drive is: I would be stunned if more than two could explain exactly what value that represents. Jobs told his audience that 5GB could hold 1,000 songs. So it meant that most people could put their complete music library onto one mp3 player that could actually fit in their jeans pocket.

I'm going to share 10 secrets of a Steve Jobs presentation with you. It will help you give what Apple's presentation software *Keynote* calls "beautiful presentations," - the kind that will have your audience whispering or roaring WOW. What that means to you is, you'll be able to

- ☐ build credibility and position yourself as confident, intelligent, and entertaining.

- ☐ forge bonds with key decision makers.

- ☐ motivate employees.

- ☐ build greater rapport with today's customer.

- ☐ correct damaging misconceptions.

- ☐ launch a successful campaign or product.

- ☐ inspire and guide a sales team.

1. The Ultimate Headline

You need an ultimate headline to grab people's attention. You also need an ultimate headline to make it easy for your audience to spread your message around the world. Make sure your ultimate headline is Twitter friendly and headline worthy. In 2007, when Jobs said, "Today Apple reinvents the phone," he showed salespeople worldwide how to help an audience write and speak about their Apple experience. The iPhone was heralded by the media as a reinvention of the phone – just what Jobs said. Maybe that's why Apple's current CEO, Tim Cook said, "The new iPad is the ultimate poster-child of the post-PC world." Isn't it funny that the media referred to it as "the ultimate poster child"?

2. The Evil Enemy

Jobs always picked an enemy. That enemy was usually time, cost, pain, the competition, or complacency against change. He was not afraid to pick a fight with his own products. When he launched the iPad2 he said, "What have we learned? What can we improve?" Then he went on to explain how the iPad 2 was better than the first iPad. He said it had a completely new design, the graphics were nine times faster, and it had double the processing speed. When he did this he positioned Apple as a forward thinking company that not only stayed ahead of the competition, but also saw way beyond every success it enjoyed.

3. The Eloquence of Easy

Jobs' speeches and presentations usually adopted the rule of three because an audience remembers things easily in three's. Think about The Three Stooges, ABC, 123, Three Wise Men, and Charlie's Angels. Count to three – one, two, three. There's an easy rhythm when you say it, but the rhythm breaks when you say one, two, three, four.

When Jobs spoke to the students at Stanford University in 2005 he said, "Today I want to tell you three stories from my life." When he told his audience about the iPad 2 years later he said it was, "thinner, lighter, and faster." Philip Schiller, Apple's senior vice president of Worldwide Marketing compared the iPad Air to the iPad in 2013. He said it was "thinner, lighter, and more powerful." Your audience will appreciate you more if you keep things to three points in your speech or presentation.

Easy Structure examples from Darren Kelly sources

☐   Problem and Solution

"Ladies and gentleman. Profits are up 22% this year. I'd like to explain the three reasons why, and also reassure you how and why we're on track for a major increase next year."

☐   Past, Present and Future

"Ladies and gentleman, I'd like to take you on a journey. It's our company's journey. I'll begin our story in a corner shop in London. Then, I'll take you inside the success of our billion dollar company today. Finally, I'll reveal the exciting news that will ensure our company's future success."

☐   Comparison

"Ladies and gentlemen. Our competitors believe they'll beat us this year. I disagree. Let's compare our track record and our dedication to invest and innovate against our competitors shallow promises. The comparison will excite and inspire you. The comparison will also reassure today's customer that no one can serve them better."

4. The Simple Solution

Complicating a simple thing is easy, but simplifying a complicated thing requires creativity. Jobs held the same belief especially with figures. He said Apple had sold 4 million iPhones, the equivalent of "20,000 per day" since the phone went on sale. Which figure is easier to see in your mind?

At the Kindle 2 launch in 2009, Jeff Bezos adopted the Jobs strategy for simplicity. He said, "Our vision is every book ever printed in any language in under 60 seconds." When he described the Kindle 2, Bezos didn't just say it was · 36 inches thick. That's too complicated for most people to appreciate fully. Bezos placed the Kindle 2 beside a pencil to show its thickness. That's an example of the genius of simplicity.

Two simplicity killers are jargon and clichés. If a word or words are industry jargon, please explain them. One misunderstood word can change the meaning of a sentence and a speech or presentation. That misunderstanding can mean you lose a future or current customer. You must also avoid the ear shattering effects of clichés. I've chosen some clichés to make you aware of the danger they pose for your message.

- ☐ "At the end of the day."
- ☐ "Let's face it."
- ☐ "In this day and age."
- ☐ "It's just one of those things."
- ☐ "To be honest with you."

I don't think people realise what they're communicating when they say, "to be honest with you." It really is an admission that they're not an honest person all of the time. There are many other examples of clichés that I can "sort of mention," and make you think "fair enough." "The fact of the matter" is that a cliché is "just one of those things" that can add "a load of waffle" and ruin your message!

5. The Exciting Feeling

Jobs' words were always in synch with the Apple brand. He used words like "exciting," "extraordinary," and "mesmerising." These words create WOW emotions. He called the MacBook Air, "the world's thinnest notebook." When he introduced the iPhone Jobs said "Today, we are introducing three revolutionary products. The first one is a widescreen iPod with touch controls. The second is a revolutionary mobile phone. And the third is a breakthrough Internet communications device…an iPod, a phone, an Internet communicator…an iPod, a phone, are you getting it? These are not three devices. This is one device!" The words "revolutionary" and "breakthrough" helped create excitement and suspense. Do words matter? Yes they do.

Certain words can alienate people and dampen enthusiasm in meetings, speeches, and presentations, and other words can inspire understanding, trust, happiness, and success.

Please read the following words aloud.

- ☐ Invite
- ☐ Discover
- ☐ Save
- ☐ Money

10. Passion for Promotion

- ☐ Results
- ☐ Celebrate
- ☐ Unite
- ☐ Easy
- ☐ New
- ☐ Fun
- ☐ Safe
- ☐ Imagine
- ☐ Excite
- ☐ Benefit
- ☐ Guarantee
- ☐ Love
- ☐ Digital
- ☐ Indulge
- ☐ You
- ☐ Delicious
- ☐ Customised

- [ ] Evoke

- [ ] Adore

- [ ] Refresh

- [ ] Surprise

- [ ] Luxury

- [ ] Happiness

- [ ] Modern

- [ ] Striking

- [ ] Style

- [ ] Perfect

- [ ] Saviour

How do these words make you feel? Isn't it true that every word you use has an emotion attached to it? You'll notice the power of emotive words the next time you walk into an Apple store and you're offered a seat at the *Genius Bar*. They make no claims to be geniuses and it's not a bar like Cheers; the real genius is in the name. As Jobs said, "That's how we think about these things. We started with the iPod, then we added the iPhone, and then the iPad. Every one has been a blockbuster." Do your words create the blockbuster effect?

6. The Glorious Vision

Jobs' presentations were big on visuals and short on text. Many of them had music, photos, and movies, but they had only one theme per slide to give each message space to breathe. An average salesperson sends today's audience to sleep with screen after screen of bullet points and other clutter. Why would you want to lose people's attention; the same people you're trying to inform, persuade, or motivate? You want your audience to understand and retain your message. Their emotional responses will be deeply governed by the images you create and the colours you use.

Think about Jobs' presentations. Why did he use blue or black movie screens? Do you prefer to read white text off a blue or black movie screen, or blue or black text off a white movie screen? I think you'll find that white text on a blue or black movie screen is easier to read. If it's easier to read, the presentation is easier to understand. A green background works well when you want to create an atmosphere of honest and valued interaction. The colours I mentioned may seem conservative, but Jobs knew about the calming effect they offered his audiences. Beware of the dangerous colours and colour mixes that can offer a migraine induced turn-off. Red is renowned for stirring passion, but it's also related to war and stop lights. Blue and orange don't mix. Purple and blue are not best friends either.

7. The Everlasting Story

Jobs recognised that we were born into a world of storytellers. It's how the greatest wisdom of our ancestors and the greatest imagination of living generations are brought to life. Jobs also knew that the story is always the king in a speech or presentation, and no technical wizardry will ever transform a bad story into a great story. It was a lesson he learnt from studying Walt Disney. Mickey Mouse's creator said, "Since the beginning of mankind, the fable-tellers have not only given us entertainment, but a kind of wisdom, humor, and understanding that, like all true art, remains imperishable through the ages." That's why you must be able to tell a unique and everlasting story about your company, your products, your services, and yourself when you need to.

Jobs always offered emotional stories with a great hook, a challenge, and a choice to be made. He always gave his audience a hero with a great solution - Apple. Jobs understood the enduring power of emotion over logic because he knew that emotion

- requires less energy to understand.

- is more attractive.

- is easier to remember.

- creates a feeling of WOW.

When you tell a story, you open your audience's minds to new thoughts and possibilities. Stories have a greater long-term impact than facts and figures alone because they can be retold more easily by today's customer. The real art is to take your facts and figures and place them into a story that your audience will never forget. I'd like to show you how you can deliver a story that your audience will never forget. Do you remember when the music industry lived with worry because illegal peer-to-peer file sharing sites were thriving? Let's take the framework of the story *The Good Samaritan* and add the music industry's worries and the solution *The i Tech Guy* (Jobs) created.

I've broken the story into five parts to demonstrate how you can take today's customer to the scene of the event, show them what happened,

10. Passion for Promotion

show them why *The i Tech Guy* was so brave, show them the challenges the other people may have faced, and how you can reveal the story's main point.

It was 2003: the internet was a place approximately one second away, and if you used a search engine you could easily access peer-to-peer file sharing sites. These sites were like a free record shop. You could have any song you wanted in seconds. Straight away, you've received a picture of an easy journey to free music downloads. This picture will help you understand the challenges of the people you're about to read about. A singer's music was robbed by illegal downloaders. The robbery of the singer's copyright and royalties meant he couldn't fund his next album. Because his music lost its monetary value many PR people, song writers, executives, back-up musicians, roadies, and many more people would soon lose their jobs too.

A fully aware lawyer and an ill-informed parent ignored the singer's plight, but luckily *The i Tech Guy* decided to help him. At this point, it's wise to take your audience deeper into the story by showing them the challenges of helping the singer in despair. *The i Tech Guy* put his reputation in jeopardy because parts of the world were getting closer to morally accepting illegal music downloads. It's certainly worth pondering what excuses the lawyer and the parent may have given for ignoring the illegal downloads. Perhaps the lawyer was too busy studying for their intellectual property exams, and the parent was happy saving money on music. When you ask these hypothetical questions, you may actually arrive at the truth.

It's time now for the major point of the story. Isn't it true that the lawyer and the parent were concerned about what would've happened had they decided to help? However, isn't it also true that *The i Tech Guy* was more concerned about what would've happened had he not decided to help? *The i Tech Guy* saw the damage illegal downloads were doing to the music industry and music lovers. The quality was poor, there were no album covers, and you could never call illegal services reliable. *The i Tech Guy* saved the singer and other singers with an Apple Product that he called the *iTunes store*. People were offered the chance to buy authentic, legal, and better quality versions of the music they loved. It restored the value of music and revitalised the careers of Bob Dylan and The Beatles – great singers and musicians, and some of the finest ever storytellers.

8. The Power of Punchy

One of the biggest mistakes a salesperson can make is to speak or present for too long. The TED talks, which feature many experts in business, health, and science have an 18-minute rule. America's 16th president, Abraham Lincoln's, Gettysburg Address, recognised as one of the greatest speeches of all time, is only 273 words long. That's what you call a punchy speech. When Jobs spoke to the students at Stanford University in 2005 his speech was under 15 minutes long. If you plan to speak for longer think about the following. Even the most spectacular West End and Broadway shows have audience breaks to combat attention fatigue.

In 1976, the year Jobs co-founded Apple, a girl called Carol Connors was asked to co-write the words for a song to be featured in an upcoming movie about a boxer. Connors heard the music to the song, written by Bill Conti, and she started to work on the words soon after. While taking a shower one day, the words popped into her head, and she knew immediately that her song would be a hit. Connors was thrilled when she delivered the words to *Gonna Fly Now*, which became the theme to the movie *Rocky*. When the movie was released, the final version of the song contained only 30 words from the song she'd submitted. Connors soon realised that those 30 words managed to capture the ethos of the whole movie. The song received an Oscar nomination and topped the American Billboard Charts in July, 1977.

Connors said the song paid for her house. This story demonstrates that one unnecessary word can be the difference between a good speech or presentation and one that creates a feeling of WOW.

9. The Gorgeous Goodbye

Jobs was a master at ending his speeches and presentations. He knew that the end is not the place to add fresh information because it confuses an audience. It's a place to remind them of the key points of your speech or presentation, and it's your opportunity to drive them towards action. Ask yourself, 'What's the next step I want my audience or today's customer to accomplish or think about after I've spoken?' Whatever it is; make sure it's as engaging, and as passionate as the rest of your speech or presentation. If you're not on top of your game, you'll leave them feeling flat.

You can simply summarize the key points: that way, anyone who has switched off mentally (to tweet or daydream) can capture the big picture of what you said. Who can forget Jobs' words at the end of his speech to the students of Stanford University in 2005 – "Stay Hungry. Stay Foolish. Thank you all very much."

10. The Insanity of WOW

Jobs often used the words "insanely great." If you want to give an insanely great speech or presentation you must rehearse it. Rehearsal means repetition and refinement. Some people find that hard to do. Jobs rehearsed his speeches and presentations for days, but average salespeople don't have the energy or the dedication to create WOW. If you have a captive audience why would you ruin such a golden opportunity to promote your ideas, products, or services? Let's look at six insanely great rehearsal tips to help you perfect your presentation.

- Keep your speech or presentation a secret. In 2002, I walked into the room of a major company and the technical person was checking my presentation on the screen. The problem was that the audience could see my presentation. It killed the suspense. Always make sure your audience never sees your presentation before you speak.

- Rehearse your speech or presentation in the venue you're going to speak at. It offers you the opportunity to get a feel for the room. You can walk on stage and test your microphone is good enough. If the volume on the microphone is too loud, your voice will distort. If the volume is too low, some people may not hear you. A great microphone is essential because it prevents you from straining your voice, and it also allows you to have more vocal variety, so you can move from a normal delivery to a whisper and still be heard. It's worth asking someone else to test the microphone while you sit in different seats in the venue to check that everyone will be able to hear and see you. If some people are unable to hear and see you properly it may be game over for you connecting with them.

- Delivery. If you plan on reading from notes, you'll need to maintain as much eye contact as possible with your audience. Make sure your text size is big enough for you to read it easily. If you fear losing your point on the page, you can use your index finger as a guide, or you can highlight certain parts of the text.

- If you decide to memorise your speech or presentation, I suggest that you don't learn it word-for-word. Many salespeople, who try to recall their speech or presentation word for word, tend to spend too much time thinking internally instead of trying to connect with their audience. It's best to remember

10. Passion for Promotion

key points that can guide your delivery. Speaking without notes like Jobs did is the most impressive way to deliver a speech or presentation, but it also takes a lot of work to be "insanely great."

☐ Get feedback from people who are not afraid to tell you the truth. You must find out if your speech or presentation flows with energy, education, and entertainment. If you lose your audience for too long at a weak point in your speech or presentation you may have wasted your time on stage.

☐ Create your own warm up routine. It may include deep breathing, a licking of your lips, gentle humming, and singing. If you're stressed you may clench your fists and relax them, shake your arms, and tap your feet. You may also visualise a great performance. The Oscar winning singer Cher told me that she has a CD with her vocal warm ups on it, and she uses it before every show. You may not be singing to sold-out arenas, but you must get your voice and body warmed up and your mind ready to speak.

There's one final rule for insanely great rehearsing. Your aim is to rehearse enough times to give you confidence in your performance. However, you must be ready to deliver your speech or presentation as if you're delivering it for the first time – as if you've never rehearsed it – that's the art of WOW.

When Things Go Wrong

You must be prepared to deal with the little or big things that can go wrong in a speech or presentation. Think about Chesley "Sully" Sullenberger, the pilot who landed an airplane on the Hudson River in New York City on 15 January, 2009. He said he forced calm on himself when birds flew into his engines and defeated technology. If technology breaks down remember that you're only giving a speech or a presentation. You're not responding to a life or death emergency. Show your audience you're a professional and bring your speech or presentation to life without your planned visuals if you must. Here are just a few examples of how things can go wrong and how you can prevent them happening or recover from them.

- A corrupt PowerPoint file won't open. I suggest you use a recovery tool for the file. A better option is to create other backup methods. You can use an online storage programme such as iCloud, or Office 365, or have your presentation on at least two memory sticks.

- People look drowsy. It may not be your communication. The room temperature may be too high. The temperature should be gauged against the size of the room and the number of people in it.

- No equipment. The venue doesn't have the equipment you need. I suggest you use your own remote control to display your PowerPoint presentation instead of using the down arrow on a computer. Using the arrow restricts your movement on stage and it forces you to look at your computer. If you possess your own remote control you don't have to worry if the venue doesn't have one. Just remember to check the battery level. You may think I'm being too fussy, but I suggest you take your own laptop too in case the venue's laptop doesn't want to work.

- The laptop goes to sleep or pings unexpectedly. You must turn off the sleep mode and email alerts, instant messages, and other pop-up windows.

☐   Your mobile phone rings. Leave it backstage before you speak.

☐   You can't read the font. Make sure you check the version of PowerPoint that the venue uses. If you use text from a later version of PowerPoint you may have a problem. Put Microsoft PowerPoint viewer 2007 on your memory stick and use it if need be.

☐   Your information becomes redundant due to an event that happens right before your speech or presentation. Take out the redundant bits and speak less.

> *"The single biggest problem in communication is the illusion that it has taken place."*
>
> **George Bernard Shaw**

The Laughing Matter

Have you ever found yourself smiling or laughing in a group without knowing the reason why? That's because laughter is infectious. It's the reason people will always pay more to be entertained than educated. The former British prime minister, Margaret Thatcher said that America's 40th president, Ronald Reagan used humour to achieve a purpose more meaningful than laughter. He used it to make people feel comfortable and to suppress any tension during tough negotiations. Fans of *The Iron Lady* say she was no stranger to humour herself: they point to her first speech in front of America's 39th president, Jimmy Carter in the White House in 1979. They say she achieved rapport with her audience with her gentle joke about George Washington being a British subject for the first forty years of his life. She also admitted that British and American relations could've gotten off to a better start. Her fans say she sent her audience into a fit of giggles when she apologised for ruining the day for the American Secretary of State. When she arrived at the airport, he was watching the Washington Redskins play the Dallas Cowboys. She blamed herself for the Redskins loss. *The Iron Lady* and *humour* are not words you normally see together, but her fans say at least she knew the value of humour.

Humour suspends negative thoughts and places your audience in a receptive state. Have you ever noticed that funny people seem to have more friends? That's because humour disarms mistrust and negativity, especially if it's self-deprecating. America's 35th president, John F. Kennedy said, "I'll always be remembered as the man who accompanied Jackie Kennedy to Paris." When Kennedy was asked if he spent much time reading a newspaper after becoming president, he replied, "I am reading it more and enjoying it less." This skill of humour was also used by Abraham Lincoln. Lincoln once responded to a question about his integrity by saying, "If I were two-faced, would I be wearing this one?"

It's a fact that humour improves your audience's ability to listen. Shakespeare used comic relief to lower people's mental barriers and to balance the serious issues with a smile. Take note of the word "relief" in comic relief. That's what your audience craves, so please don't just rely on logic and reason alone. Humour works because we laugh at the prospect of humour coming; we laugh at the person offering the humour; we laugh at the humour; and we laugh when we're reminded of the humour.

At the *Roast of Representative* speech on 20 September, 2005, Barack Obama told the audience that Rahm Emmanuel, a former senior advisor to Bill Clinton was "an inspiration for the character Tony Soprano." Obama was able to poke fun at Emmanuel because he was a friend. His audience also understood that Obama is the type of person who likes to poke fun at himself. At the *Alfred E. Smith Memorial Dinner* on 16 October, 2008, Obama poked fun at his media image by telling his audience that contrary to a belief, he wasn't born in a manger, but on the planet Krypton to a father called Jorel. In his *Take Back America* speech on 14 June, 2006, he told his audience about the first time he got involved in politics. He said people would laugh at his name and call him "Alabama" and "Yo Mama." Obama showed that when you want to have fun at another person's expense, it's best to prove that you're able to joke about your own failures, quirky characteristics, and experiences. It's also best that your audience feels you're not being mean, and that your joke is the sort of gentle fun they may have with their own friends.

You must, however, safeguard yourself against using humour that may come back to haunt you. If you've got permission to poke fun, it's okay to joke about a person's minor personality flaws. But when you attack their physical appearance, you must remember that you're also attacking people in your audience who look similar. You'll also offend people who consider your remark to be that of a bully. The most important lesson for you when using humour is, "when in doubt, don't." Never take a gamble on humour unless you're sure. The best way to gauge if you can use humour for a certain audience is to answer these questions before you use humour:

☐ Is the humour honestly funny and imaginative?

☐ Does the humour match my personality?

☐ Is the humour appropriate for the occasion?

☐ Will my audience understand and appreciate the humour easily?

☐   Will my audience find the humour tasteful?

☐   If my humour was typed on a giant outdoor billboard, or on the internet, would it please or embarrass me?

A friend of mine who works for a leading international bank watched a famous comedian on DVD. He thought he could borrow the jokes that the comedian's audience loved. I asked him if he was trying to commit career suicide. He stared at me with a blank expression. I believe humour is essential for any speech or presentation, but you're better off introducing it gradually if you're new to it. Some comedians rehearse their routines for 10 years before they get their break. Why would you think you can do it after 10 minutes?

People always ask me, "How do you find humorous things to speak about?" I say that humour is all around you if you just pay attention. Having a sense of humour means you appreciate the humorous side of events in your life. As George Bernard Shaw said, "My way of joking is to tell the truth. It's the funniest joke in the world."

> *"Inspire today's customer's heart,
> and you'll inspire their mind."*
>
> **Darren Kelly**

The First Lady of WOW

When Michelle Obama spoke at the Democratic National Convention in 2012, she became a megastar. The First Lady, no longer a reluctant political spouse, arrived on stage as the most popular star in the 2012 presidential campaign. She demonstrated WOW with ease. Even the number of tweets sent per minute of her speech (28,000) beat Bill

Clinton (22,000). As soon she appeared on the blue carpeted stage women wanted to know who made her pink, gold, and blue-grey sleeveless dress. A young African-American designer called Tracy Reese made the custom dress which she matched with pink pumps by J. Crew. Are clothes important for a salesperson? Absolutely! The much admired and stylish First Lady managed to look chic with a common touch. Her speech was as inspiring as it was humbling. It was high on sound-bite, but also high on substance and full of relatable emotions.

How did Obama manage to win so many people over? The answer is simple. She was honest and passionate. When you're honest, you build rapport. You can only persuade an audience after you build rapport. Ask yourself how you feel towards a woman who expresses gratitude and praise for genuine heroes, who expresses natural worries about her children, who loves her partner regardless of what profession he's in, who admits to motherly tiredness, and who tells you about her father's illnesses and his struggle to pay the bills. When someone opens their heart to reveal the private issues and thoughts that you experience and feel too, you feel a bond. That's what Obama did.

Have you ever watched an advertisement for a boxing match or pop concert on pay per view TV? Isn't it true that the advertisement never mentioned the price at the start? It gave you the value and created that value by building suspense until the words and images reached fever pitch. It was at the moment of highest emotional impact that the advertisement revealed the price. Because you may have been logically and emotionally persuaded, the price became almost irrelevant if you wanted to see it. Obama did the same thing in her speech. She created rapport with logic and emotion before she asked for the votes her husband needed. Can you imagine if Obama had walked out on stage and said, "Barack did this and Barack did that"? It would've seemed like a gloating list. Her first challenge was to provide the reasons behind his work. When you offer the reasons and value for your actions before you make a request, your words have greater credibility. The speech was by far her most political, most passionate, and most poignant one. It helped her husband win a second-term as president.

HELLO PROFIT Challenge 10

Reignite Your Passion

You can't expect people to have a feeling of WOW about your ideas, products, and services if you're not passionate about them. You can't fake passion in a speech or presentation. I suggest that you honestly reignite or strengthen your passion for selling with WOW every day. Apart from your salary, bonus, and commission, can you list eight things you love about your current job?

They can be that you love

- meeting new people every day.
- being tested with a challenge every day that helps you grow.
- helping others.
- the freedom to choose your career limits.
- working in a team.
- discovering how other people work.

☐   learning about other cultures and industries.

☐   your company's products and services.

Take your time to complete this passion list. If you find yourself struggling to complete the list, you can ask a friend or a partner to help you, or to share their thoughts. They may mention something that you really enjoy, but you don't consciously think about. Take your list of the seven things you love about your current job, and put them in order of preference, with your favourite at number one and your least favourite at number eight. You'll discover the real reasons why you enjoy selling.

Many salespeople say that their salary, bonus, and commission are their main reasons to go to work, but it goes deeper than that. When you discover or rediscover what your main reasons are, you can sell with **WOW** every day. This creates the sort of passion, control, and insight that powered Jobs' success. Please take the time to read this passion list for the next 21 days to reaffirm the feelings of passion you possess and need for selling success. Jobs has been hailed as a genius, entrepreneur, and inventor. Many people forget that he was also one of the world's greatest ever salespeople – his passion was the foundation for his ability to sell with **WOW**.

11. Habit for Harmony

*"We are what we repeatedly do.
Excellence, then,
is not an act,
but a habit."*

Aristotle

- ☐ Habit of WOW
- ☐ Get Better with WOW
- ☐ WOW for Life
- ☐ Kelly's Sales Ladder™
- ☐ The Scent of Success
- ☐ The Pink Habit
- ☐ Refreshing Inspiration
- ☐ The Intimacy of WOW

- ☐ **HELLO PROFIT Challenge II**

    The Happy Habit

Habit of WOW

You can't sell with WOW unless you adopt the habit of WOW. This habit is a regular action that thrills, excites, and amazes today's customer. You can't be a great salesperson Monday to Thursday, but decide to sell half-heartedly on Friday. Today's customer loves consistent quality, and that's why a great salesperson sells with WOW every day. A great salesperson is consistent because they thrive on the buzz of a satisfied and profitable customer. Today's customer's smiles, emails of appreciation, recommendations, and repeat orders, offer them fuel for their success.

In his bestselling book *My Autobiography*, Sir Alex Ferguson made a great point that's relevant for every salesperson. In the chapter about his former Manchester United captain, Roy Keane, he referred to habit as being essential for the making of a player. Baseball legend Joe Di Maggio was a master of habit. Di Maggio was inducted into the Baseball Hall of Fame in 1955. He was once asked why he performed at the highest level in games that didn't matter. He replied, "Because there is always some kid who may be seeing me for the first time." DiMaggio, who was once married to Marilyn Monroe said, "I owe him my best." A great salesperson knows that all it takes is one lapse in concentration, one mistake, one piece of sloppy service, or one unresolved dispute to destroy all their hard work. Doesn't today's customer deserve your best all the time? When you develop your habit of WOW you'll satisfy today's customer regularly and automatically. Isn't WOW a worthy habit that offers harmony for profit?

Get Better with WOW

One woman understood the words *habit of WOW long* before other salespeople did. Estée Lauder was born on 1 July, 1908 in Queens, New York. Her real name was Josephine Esther Mentzer, and her immigrant parents called her Esty for short. This quickly changed to Estée because of her father's strong accent. She married Joseph Lauter in her twenties, and they adopted the original spelling of the family name, which is Lauder. Lauder learnt how to serve every customer with WOW while working at her father's hardware store as a child.

However, her Uncle John's chemist held even more excitement for the young girl. She marvelled at the way he created creams, lotions, and fragrances. He educated her in the art of having a beauty regime, and she was soon selling her uncle's products to all her best friends. Marriage in 1930 didn't slow Lauder's love for her career. She seemed to work even harder. Her own flawless skin worked as an advert for the products she sold, but she wanted to sell her products and advice in a big department store. Lauder knew her market, and she wanted to be in the best place to reach them. In 1948, after over 50 attempts, she secured a counter at Saks on Fifth Avenue, New York. Lauder studied the location of counter spaces at Saks, like an investor does to a major property. She discovered that the majority of women turned right after entering the department store. Lauder didn't care what the reasons were; she just knew her counter had to be positioned on the right, so it was the first thing a customer saw and walked towards.

WOW for Life

Time magazine featured Lauder's story in 1998. It praised her products, but said Lauder as a salesperson was better. She "simply outworked" her competitors. Lauder once explained her success by saying she never worked a day in her life without selling. She knew that it's not what you do once in a while that helps you achieve success, but what you do every day. Lauder prepared, prospected, qualified, handled objections, and sold successfully, every day. She was a consistent go-getter who didn't see the slumps that an average salesperson sees.

Lauder took pleasure in visiting department stores to educate every salesperson in how to offer free facials, offer free samples, and help every customer choose what worked best for them. She surprised her sales teams when she introduced training to help them sell female beauty products to men. Women across the world were soon receiving WOW appreciation from their husbands, boyfriends, and admirers because one woman believed that all women deserved to feel beautiful.

Kelly's Sales Ladder™

Imagine Estée Lauder had used *Kelly's Sales Ladder*™ to measure her habit of WOW. Where do you think she would be at the start and at the end of every day?

1. I sold.

2. I will sell.

3. I can sell.

4. I think I can sell.

5. I might sell.

6. I think I might sell.

7. What can I sell?

8. I wish I could sell.

9. I don't know how to sell.

10. I can't sell.

11. It won't sell.

12. It's impossible to sell.

13. It's a stupid thing to sell.

14. There's no guarantee I will sell.

15. I always fail to sell.

16. I don't care if I sell.

17. Let other people sell it.

18. If it sells, it sells.

19. It will sell itself.

20. It might sell itself.

Your success is based solely on your consistent results. Your consistency is affected by your habit of WOW. Your habit is affected by your thoughts. Your aim should be to wake up every day on rung number two of the ladder and go to sleep every night on rung number one. This habit of WOW will help you achieve enduring success.

The Scent of Success

Despite Lauder's extraordinary global success, perhaps the greatest story about her habit of WOW is how she connected with French women. After her counter opened at Harrods, London in 1960, other stores like Selfridges followed. However, Lauder struggled to gain a counter at The Galeries Lafayette, an upmarket French department store in Paris. However, Lauder's habit of WOW that helped her get a counter at Saks gave her a WOW idea. She took a bottle of her Youth Dew perfume and spilled it on the floor of the Parisian department store. The store's procurement manager, who had previously ignored Lauder had to pay attention because every customer demanded it.

It's worth thinking more deeply about Lauder's habit of WOW. She didn't become arrogant after her American and British successes. She didn't expect the people of France to race to her door and beg her for her perfume. Lauder knew that the biggest problem that most companies have is obscurity: no one knows who they are, or what they represent. Too many companies design a great website, create great product, spend a fortune on inept marketing, and wonder why no one is buying from them. The reason is simple – they don't know how to sell with WOW. Here is the brutal reality. There are new competitors entering your market every day. They want your business or a slice of it. They don't care how long you've been in business. They don't care that your customer loves and trusts you. They want your customer. So you must sell with WOW every day to today's customer. Because someone might be ready today to drop their product at your customer's door just like Lauder did in Paris years ago.

Lauder was 97-years-old when she died in 2004 at her home in New York. People listened to her and bought from her because they knew she cared every time and every day. It was this habit that made a queen of beauty an inspiration to women and men all over the world.

The Pink Habit

In 2009, Estée Lauder Companies, Inc appointed its CEO, Fabrizio Freda as its president. Italian born Freda understands how to sell in a diverse global market. This is certainly a different market to the one Lauder started from her kitchen table, but the same skills apply. When Freda spoke about 2011 being an outstanding year for Estée Lauder Companies, Inc. he said they achieved "record sales," and "strong sales growth" in every region and category of product. 2013 was a superb year with Freda reporting that the company achieved a record breaking $10 billion in net sales and 15.2% operating margin. That's what you call WOW.

Selling with WOW takes on even greater power when you sell a vision to save people's lives. One of Estée Lauder Companies' consistent efforts is their support of the Breast Cancer Awareness (BCA) life-saving campaign. Lauder's late daughter in law, Evelyn Lauder established the Breast Cancer Research Foundation in 1993. Evelyn Lauder also co-created the recognized symbol of breast cancer awareness - the Pink Ribbon.

Breast cancer affects one in eight women worldwide; that's one in eight families. The campaign encourages women to go beyond awareness to get diagnosed early. Their mission is to help eradicate the disease. Its 2013 theme communicated its mission clearly - *Let's Defeat Breast Cancer. We're Stronger Together.* The website www.bcacampaign.com features *Circles of Strength*. It inspires people to create proactive teams to offer support for a person with breast cancer. In 1995 the *New York Times* applauded Evelyn Lauder's organisational skills, and when she died in 2011 the Breast Cancer Research Foundation praised her dedication that never wavered. She sold the world on the idea that recovery from breast cancer is possible because she'd survived it in 1989. Today, the Breast Cancer Research Foundation sells a vision of a happy life beyond breast cancer. That's the kind of selling that deserves the greatest accolade of WOW.

> *"Powerful indeed is the empire of habit."*
>
> **Publilius Syrus**

Refreshing Inspiration

I once asked a salon owner why he was so successful. He said that every customer was treated like a £100,000 customer. That's the average lifetime value he put on every customer relationship. It included the value of what every customer told their friends about his salon. Now think about this. How do you think his team act today when they think about their £100,000 customer, as opposed to an £80 per haircut customer? This is a brilliant mind-set to help you develop the habit of WOW. You should do the same. Treat today's customer with a benchmark of their lifetime value, and you'll have them for a lifetime.

He also said he was very quick to handle the smallest customer upset. He said that when trouble brews with today's customer it could be "their fault, your fault, or someone else's fault. The main thing to understand is that you hold an opportunity to refresh or terminate the relationship. It's up to you." He made an amazing point. When today's customer makes a complaint it may be the best thing that can happen to you. The natural thing for most companies is to dismiss complaints or begrudgingly resolve them. But think about this for a moment: if today's customer complains, they may be giving you notice of a problem that may arise later for every other customer. No company is perfect, and sometimes you can be too close to your company to see the obvious. A customer complaint may just be your saviour one day. It can create a WOW moment.

Please don't treat complaints procedures as a boring must do job. Treat them as a habit of WOW - an exciting and integrated part of your customer solution. In fact, I'd go as far as to say that you should greet your complaining customer at the door with a bouquet of flowers. Let me explain why. Today's customer may take you for granted, but when a problem arises, and you solve it quickly, their appreciation grows. This makes their perception of your value grow. Take every complaint and harness its power; it's great for profit.

> *"Success is an everyday thing."*
>
> **Darren Kelly**

The Intimacy of WOW

For a company to sell with WOW every leader must develop the habit of WOW. They must stay in touch with an ever evolving customer mind-set in the good and bad times. I love the ethos of Paul Caplan, the President of Go Outdoors, Britain's biggest outdoor stores. Caplan insists on seeing every customer complaint. He regards it as a strategic imperative. Some leaders are foolish to think complaints never occur, and others simply dismiss them as unimportant. Caplan regards the few complaints Go Outdoors receive as feedback and a way to prove the company genuinely cares. Caplan has an incredible ability to step inside the mind of today's customer and serve them with WOW. When he walked into Sheffield's Camping and Caravanning Centre in 1996 he was supposed to buy a barbecue. Instead, he decided to buy the shop and his company began. His enthusiastic, entrepreneurial awareness helps Go Outdoors maintain the habit of WOW.

Everything the company does is designed to create consistent and irresistible value from pricing and quality to ease of purchase. It was Go Outdoors who introduced the first British smartphone-based loyalty scheme. Their customer base doesn't have to worry about keeping a plastic loyalty card. They can simply present their smartphone to a cashier to receive their loyalty discounts. Caplan's desire to innovate customer service excellence and his habit of WOW is a model for every company.

HELLO PROFIT Challenge 11

The Happy Habit

Discover if WOW is a habit for you.

☐ When was the last time you connected with your core customer base?

☐ How did you enrich their lives? Did you sell them something, answer a query, or provide a solution for a problem they had?

☐ What's the best thing they ever said about you and your company?

- [ ] What's the worst thing they ever said about you and your company?

- [ ] How do you keep the relationship fresh without being intrusive?

- [ ] How do you maintain relationships with future decision makers?

- [ ] How do you promote yourself in their sphere of influence?

- [ ] How do you promote yourself in their industry?

- [ ] How can you partner with today's customer on other projects to cement the relationship?

- [ ] What social cause is today's customer most passionate about? Are you connected with that cause? Do you support it consistently?

- [ ] Does your complaints procedure aim to rectify problems begrudgingly, or does it seek to make today's customer think "WOW"? Is this done every day?

- [ ] What action of yours hurts your relationship with today's customer? It could be a propensity for lateness, misguided confidence, or ineffective solutions. Are you prepared to change every detrimental action to create the habit of WOW?

PART 3.

12. Asking for Agreement

13. Nerve for Negotiation

14. Time for Triumph

15. Caution for Crises

WOW Forever

12. Asking for Agreement

*"Ask with urgency
and passion."*

Arthur J. Balfour

- ☐ Don't Close
- ☐ Ask with Obligation
- ☐ Ask with Trust
- ☐ Ask for Yes
- ☐ Ask without Fear
- ☐ Ask with WOW
- ☐ Ask after Rejection

- ☐ **HELLO PROFIT Challenge 12**

  Better Asking

Don't Close

You can't sell with WOW if you don't ask for an agreement. Asking in this case is simply an honest request for a buying decision. Too many salespeople are afraid to ask, or they ask in a way that places the agreement above the relationship. You should never focus on *closing* the sale. I'm not trying to be different when I say *closing* is the most dangerous word I hear an average salesperson use. *Closing* suggests the end of a relationship and suggests today's customer will be passed over to another department forever. It also suggests the interaction has only ever been about that transaction. I disagree with every sales trainer and average salesperson who relies on outdated, pushy, and predatory *closes*. Am I being too harsh? I don't think so. If your job is to build trust, offer value, and reach an agreement, why do you need to be deceitful?

Today's customer is fed up of hearing misleading and pushy options that favour a salesperson's commission. The shady *closes* of yester year are spoken by an average salesperson who doesn't understand the new reality. The pushy sale of today leads to regret, anger, and dissatisfaction tomorrow. This results in the loss of today's customer tomorrow. Think about it. It's not just about making the sale: it's about opening the relationship. You want today's customer to have no regrets. If they feel hoodwinked they'll tell at least 10 people: in today's word of mouth platform on social media, unscrupulous practices will kill your business. I've met some of the most amazing, professional, and honest salespeople who kill their careers with the cheesy lines they learnt from well-intentioned, but ill-informed sales trainers. These lines are the equivalent of asking someone you just met if they'd like to go back to your apartment for a coffee. Please don't use them because you're a sophisticated and trustworthy professional.

I'm often approached by salespeople who are no better than deceitful manipulators. They try to create fear in my mind if I don't buy from them, or they try to make me feel obliged to buy after their lengthy self-serving presentations. When I feel manipulated I say, "I'll think about it," but I never deal with the person after that. You must never try to mis-sell today's customer. Simply follow what's in the book so far. You'll earn respect when you show respect. If you attempt to manipulate, you'll lose.

Let me explain further why I prefer to use the word *open* instead of *close*. If it's a new customer you're dealing with, an agreement is an opening of the relationship. If it's a current customer, an agreement represents the opening of another door of trust and service. This thought process keeps you from becoming complacent just because you arranged a meeting, or you made an impressive presentation. You know that nothing happens until you ask for and formalise an agreement. Please accept that you never close anything. Your job is to open the relationship and keep it open.

> "Furtherance is the agreement
> of all that is just."
>
> **Lao Tzu**

Ask with Obligation

An average salesperson fears asking for an agreement, so they fail to ask, or they ask as if they're begging for an agreement. I'm always asked why salespeople fear asking for an agreement. My answer is always the same. It's because they don't believe 100% in the value they offer.

An average salesperson belittles today's customer by bamboozling them with insider jargon and scare tactics. Your job is to offer authentic counsel, but this must be done at the right time. If you ask the right question at the wrong time you may lose an agreement. So when is the right time to ask for business to open the relationship? The answer I always give is "at the right time." It can be within a minute of meeting today's customer, or a minute before your engagement ends. It all depends on what they're thinking. Do you recognise the signals that indicate today's customer may be giving your offer serious consideration? They may be ready if they

☐ ask you about cost, payment methods, and terms.

☐ ask you about the results, materials, colours, the model, etc.

☐ break from a frown to a smile, or if they unfold their arms.

☐ start working out figures on a note pad or calculator.

☐ ask who else is using your products and services.

☐ compliment you, your company, and what you offer.

If these signals don't show up, you can try a trial open that gently suggests moving to an agreement. A trial open is a non-pressured question that builds momentum towards the main open. You should ask with ease as if it's a natural progression of a conversation to give and accept value. You don't want today's customer feeling uncomfortable. Just raise an honest request to win the business. If you do your work before you ask, you'll win the business most of the time. Don't start going shy at this point. You've worked hard, and you deserve an answer. After all, respect works both ways. You must remember that you're not an ambassador; you're a salesperson. Asking for an agreement represents about 5% of the sales process, but your planning and preparation will mean nothing if you don't do it.

> *"Many of life's failures are people who did not realise how close they were to success when they gave up."*
>
> **Thomas A. Edison**

Ask with Trust

Let's look at the trust killing words that an average salesperson uses to force today's customer into buying. They adopt the mind-set I dislike – the *close(d) one*.

- ☐ Straight Close – "I can see you like the product, when do you want delivery?"

- ☐ Assumptive Close – "Would you like the car delivered on Friday?"

- ☐ Urgent Close – "I can offer you this price until Friday because we have a special offer."

- ☐ Alternative Close - "Would you like the car in black or red?"

12. Asking for Agreement   233

- Profit and Loss Close – "Would you like to make the savings now. Would you like to reduce your losses now?"

- No Extra Value Close. "If I can get you the furry dice for free would you like to go ahead now?"

- Triple Close. "Would you like to buy X, Y, or Z?" This approach gives them a chance to stress their sensational offer against two offers of lesser value.

- Urgent and Exclusive Close. "This offer is only available to you today."

- Hand them a Pen Close. "Here; use my pen to sign."

I heard a sales trainer tell an audience they could buy his book of 200 different closes. How many do you seriously need? Do you need the "slam it down" close, the "push them against the wall" close, and the "pin em down" close? This sort of training is ridiculous. WOW isn't destructive and aggressive. It's empowering and it's enriching.

Ask for Yes

When you reach the point where you want to ask for an agreement you must revisit your value and appeal to today's customer at a deeper level.

Think about

- their journey.

- the values you share.

☐ the values your products and services offer.

☐ the competition. Compliment them, but you should recognise their weakness and say why you believe in your products and services.

☐ a positive endorsement from someone they know and trust.

☐ their number one requirement. Don't refer to price if they don't care about price. Appeal to speed of delivery if that's their number one demand. I'm not saying that price isn't important, but if you're prices are 5% cheaper than your competitor, but you deliver two weeks later, you may lose today's customer the 5% saving and more. So focus on their needs and wants.

You'll have a much better chance of getting an honest response if you establish an authentic conversation and you maintain it. You're better off having a "yes" or a "no" to your request than "I'll think it over." Many people hate telling a salesperson, "no" because they know what it's like to be rejected.

You must build enough rapport and trust with today's customer, so they feel comfortable telling you the truth. Their truth can be delivered in their words or through their body language. If you think you're wasting your time pursuing a lost cause you could say the following words. "Angie. When I ask for someone's business there are times when it's just not possible for them to agree. It can be a redundancy, budget, internal change, or timing issue. Now I'd be delighted to get a 'yes' from you, but I want you know that I respect this relationship, and I will accept a 'no' as professionally as a 'yes'. So if it's not a 'yes' today, I hope I can help you when you're ready."

There's nothing wrong with being straightforward. Why leave a meeting with today's customer with the promise of a future agreement, when they may be taking early redundancy, or their plant may be moving to India? I know they'll never reveal confidential information, but you'll get the truth from the words they say or don't say. Be straight and get an honest answer because delusions of future success won't pay your bills.

> *"What would your inner child do?*
> *You know that (s)he would ask*
> *with confidence.*
> *Lose your adult fear*
> *and ask."*
>
> **Darren Kelly**

Ask without Fear

If you still fear asking the all-important question, simply think about the value you've created and ask yourself the following questions.

- What's the worst thing that can happen if I fail?

- What's the best thing that can happen if I succeed?

- Who'll benefit most if I succeed?

- How much will I save if I succeed? What expenses would I incur chasing other business?

- How much money and time will today's customer lose if I fail?
- How urgent is the situation?
- What other choices does today's customer have if I fail?
- How easy have I made it for today's customer to make a decision?

Ask with WOW

You take steps towards opening an agreement with every word you say and type, and every picture you create. If you prepare and connect with today's customer, you'll have no problem asking for an agreement. I usually say

- "Makes sense to me. What do you think?"
- "Do you see the value?"
- "Does this make sense to you?"
- "Does that feel right?"
- "What benefit do you think you'd get if we move forward?"
- "How would you like to proceed from here?"

When I mention price, I say one of the following.

- "How does that sound to you?"

☐   "Does that seem fair?"

☐   "Does that fit your budget?"

If the answer is positive, I ask for an agreement. Today's customer is educated and price and value savvy. They'll pull back if you push. If you sell hard, you'll lose fast. Honesty is the best policy.

Ask after Rejection

If today's customer says, "No," I suggest you revisit your value and return to your request. Don't underestimate the importance of maintaining a composed and pleasant demeanour in the face of rejection. I often see the over-confident average salesperson look like a rabbit caught in the headlights of an oncoming car when they're told their incredible offer is of no value. If today's customer sees your confidence crumble, you'll never regain their confidence. You must believe in what you're selling, and show you believe in it at all times.

HELLO PROFIT Challenge 12

Better Asking

Write down 10 *Asking for Agreement* sentences that you can use in your next sales conversation or presentation. Don't rely on the clichés and banal words an average salesperson uses. These words kill any possible agreement and the relationship because today's customer has heard them so many times. They'll lose respect for you if they hear you say them. You're a unique salesperson, so you should write and memorise *Asking for Agreement* sentences that you feel comfortable saying. This will help you sell with WOW.

13. Nerve for Negotiation

*"You don't get what you deserve in life,
you get what you negotiate."*

Anonymous

- ☐ Negotiate with WOW
- ☐ Types of Negotiation
- ☐ WOW Preparation
- ☐ Selling Position with WOW
- ☐ Protect Your Concessions
- ☐ How to Offer Concessions
- ☐ Time Dangers
- ☐ Dirty Tricks
- ☐ The Agreement Fundamentals
- ☐ Don't Kill WOW

- ☐ **HELLO PROFIT Challenge 13**

    Handling the Hard Negotiator

Negotiate with WOW

You can't sell with WOW if you don't have the nerve to negotiate. Nerve in this case is simply your confident and capable mind-set: you need confidence to create an agreement that protects the relationship and your profit. Today's customer may seek a price reduction, or ask for better terms. You have three choices. You can cave in, walk away, or shape an agreement with your skills of negotiation. I suggest you adopt the third choice. Why? If you cave in to an easy discount you'll devalue your products and services. Today's customer will never want to pay the full price again. If you walk away you may lose current and future business. But if you negotiate with WOW you can improve the relationship, offer better terms for today's customer, and protect your profit. A salesperson who can't negotiate with WOW remains open to losing their company a lot of money.

The negotiation insights in this chapter have been used by salespeople to create small and big agreements and broker major political deals. You'll discover how to maximize your value and solve most problems in a negotiation. These skills and strategies will serve you well when you sell a product, a service, an idea, or even your family home.

Types of Negotiation

There are two main types of negotiation – cooperative and competitive. In a cooperative negotiation, your goal with today's customer is to

☐ clarify the issues.

☐ examine the extent of the issues.

☐ analyse the causes of the issues.

☐ create fair-minded solutions for profit.

You must help today's customer understand your value. You must also understand their value. This is important for two reasons. You don't want to have any resentment on either side after the agreement is made. In his brilliant book *Playing to Win: The Autobiography*, Wigan Football Club owner Dave Whelan recalled a negotiation in a rest room with one of Britain's retail kings. Whelan was in the middle of a negotiation with the former Morrisons supermarket leader, Sir Ken Morrison when he needed a toilet break. Morrison and Whelan finalised the agreement in the rest room. Because the agreement was struck with professionalism and trust, Whelan and Morrison developed a friendship. As Whelan's business grew he was able to seek Sir Ken Morrison's advice and reach other business agreements with him. This is a classic example of where you should negotiate with the lifetime value of the relationship in mind. Think cooperation and collaboration before coercion. I know it's easier to say, "We don't negotiate on the price because our price is fixed," but that's a cop out. If you want to reach the top in sales, you must negotiate with WOW. It's up to you as an expert negotiator to steer every conversation to a level of trust and harmony. This is different from a competitive negotiation – one in which the long-term relationship has little value.

"If you win negotiations with greed, you'll soon have no one to negotiate with. Think growth; not greed."

Darren Kelly

WOW Preparation

Preparation for negotiation with WOW requires sharp analysis. You must calculate every potential outcome. It's essential that you know the answers to the following questions.

- ☐ What's my primary goal, and why is it so important?
- ☐ What's my ideal outcome?
- ☐ How will I calculate my success?
- ☐ What am I willing to negotiate on?
- ☐ What am I not willing to negotiate on?
- ☐ What are the internal challenges (political and operational) I may face in my company?
- ☐ What are the internal challenges (political and operational) today's customer may face in their company or household?
- ☐ What alternatives do I have if I don't reach my goal?
- ☐ Are these alternatives good or bad?
- ☐ Which alternatives are the best?
- ☐ What would make me believe I created an equitable agreement?
- ☐ Is it a one-off negotiation, or do we have time to discuss it later?

- [ ] What are the roadblocks to an equitable agreement?
- [ ] Will a third party be required to break a possible deadlock?
- [ ] Do I know today's customer's negotiation style?
- [ ] What's the purchase and negotiation history between today's customer, my company, and me?
- [ ] How will we communicate away from the bargaining table before and after the negotiation?
- [ ] Do I or does today's customer have the most power?
- [ ] Do we have rapport to build a cooperative foundation?
- [ ] What's today's customer's primary goal, and how does it differ from mine?
- [ ] Why is their primary goal so important to them?
- [ ] What's their authority to complete an agreement?
- [ ] What choices does today's customer have to reach their goal?
- [ ] What standards will I use to test, validate, and evaluate their evidence?
- [ ] Am I focussed to avoid prejudice and opinion?
- [ ] Am I focussed to avoid speculation and early conclusions?
- [ ] How will I respond to threats?

- ☐ What alternatives does today's customer have if they don't reach an agreement?
- ☐ Are there any subtle and buried clues as to their true intentions?
- ☐ Can I position my offer as unique – not just my products and services, but my integrity?
- ☐ Do I have proof that an agreement I desire has worked elsewhere?
- ☐ Am I willing to walk away if an agreement isn't right?
- ☐ Can I authentically persuade with clear and precise evidence?
- ☐ Will failure to reach an agreement thwart future agreements?
- ☐ Will we sign straight away, or will we require approval from other people?
- ☐ Do I have an off-site support team to analyse intricate details?
- ☐ How complex will the negotiation be?
- ☐ If it's not a group negotiation, who's the best person to be my support from the outside looking in? Can I call them when I need them?
- ☐ How do I protect myself from being overconfident?
- ☐ Have I given too much respect to today's customer's title, expertise, and education?

Your goal at this stage is to prepare your questions, so you can have a confident and educated conversation. Don't treat the negotiation like an interrogation. You should avoid asking compound, leading, and accusatory questions that can hinder a possible *One-Win* scenario. Be careful not to place too much trust in your intuition. An average salesperson trusts their intuition in a negotiation. They're not always right. If you prepare, you can deal with the facts. That means you won't leave yourself open to difficult terms and conditions hidden under a pile of legal terminology.

Selling Position with WOW

Before you negotiate, you should restate your value proposition. This is called your *Selling Position*. You must include everything of measurable value, so today's customer understands and appreciates your value. This can include after-sales support, payment type and terms, lead-time, length of contract, penalties in contract, size of order, specifications, cooperation, etc. Don't focus on the price only because you'll regret it later on.

Selling with WOW is based on mutual respect and trust. You deserve an equitable return for the value you offer. You must be prepared to get it. If today's customer suggests a price, simply respond that it will depend on a number of factors. Today's customer may seek to destroy your unique proposition to get a better price: don't react. The better prepared you are, the easier the negotiation will be.

Protect Your Concessions

Every concession has a consequence. It may set a precedent, or it may offer a perception that you're a weak negotiator. It may also lead to today's customer demanding a quick result; meaning you'll never get the opportunity to sell your real value. This isn't a smart thing for future relations. When you concede a concession, you change the dynamic of the relationship. The WOW concession rule is that you give away nothing for nothing. You must get something for everything. If you give things away too cheaply, today's customer won't respect them. They'll always wonder if they could've got a better deal.

You must also protect your individual prices in an overall project, or you may find yourself having little or no profit at all. Imagine you offer to bake a person's wedding cake. Your price is £500, which is made up of £330 for your time, talent, and experience, £150 for the ingredients and packaging, and £20 for storage and delivery. Today's customer offers to buy the ingredients themselves and collect the cake too. Now they've got a figure of £330 that they'll try to negotiate on. So what do you do? You know in your heart that they'll probably struggle to deliver the ingredients on time and collect the cake as agreed. These issues will add more time to the project.

You have a duty to make them aware that you'll bake the cake at a certain time, and that any delays in their ordering of the ingredients may add extra cost to your time. They may believe they can save themselves money in the process: in fact, they run the risk of adding time and hassle to the job and paying £500 for your time only. You must make sure that they understand the issue, so that they're happy to revert to the original price. You can make a concession for payment terms, or offer a discount on future purchases. But please know your value: don't sell yourself and today's customer into unnecessary aggravation.

When you give a concession make sure you attach a condition to it. Say, "I'll give you this and in return I'd like that," or "I can reduce the price by 10 per cent if you buy all your family birthday cakes from me this year." Think about other ways you can openly and honestly trade concessions in every negotiation you enter. Can you increase a selling price on other items, reduce a contractual discount, get paid faster, change a previous special deal, remove a loss maker from a current agreement, update your overall price structure, clear obsolete stock, or upsell higher margin products and services? There are many authentic ways to trade valuable concessions that protect and improve your profit.

How to Offer Concessions

☐ Never concede a concession until today's customer has agreed to buy.

☐ Never be the first person in the negotiation to name a price.

☐ Never negotiate against yourself. If you do make an offer, you should pause and count to ten. Let today's customer speak first.

☐ If they ask, "Is that the best you can do?" revisit the maximum value of your concession. Don't just toss it away.

☐ Never fall foul of the law of unfair reciprocity. The law implies that today's customer does something small for you, and you do something big for them. Don't over compromise when today's customer compromises. Make it a like for like concession to create a *One-Win* agreement.

☐ Never suggest figures like, "between £500 and £600." Today's customer will offer you £500. They won't think £600: you wouldn't either.

☐   Never let sales fatigue force you to accept their first offer. Today's customer may sense your willingness to cave in and may try to push you further.

☐   Be ready to walk away. You'll get a better agreement if today's customer understands you hold options.

☐   Restate your value and suggest you'll refund any measurable difference if they show you an offer from your competitor. However, make sure your value is still higher than your competitor's value.

☐   Help today's customer discover their hidden concessions. You may spot some value they never thought about offering you.

☐   Pause before you agree to a concession. Make today's customer understand you've considered it carefully before you agree to it. Don't give it away too cheaply.

☐   Never assume your concession isn't valuable. Just because you don't like the carpets in the house you're selling doesn't mean today's customer doesn't value them at £800.

Time Dangers

You've heard the saying, "Timing is everything." This is very important in a negotiation. An average salesperson breaks into a cold sweat when today's customer asks them to call on the last Friday in the month to finalise an agreement. At 4.50pm on that Friday they know today's customer will push for many more concessions than if they'd arranged the meeting for 10am the previous Monday morning. Here are some golden rules for timing.

- Never disclose your time limit. "I've got until midnight" or "I think we're close" weaken your power to negotiate.

- Try and find today's customer's time limit.

- Spend most of your time listening and asking precise questions.

- Never disclose that you depend on the sale.

- Take time to refresh and renew your energy if the negotiation drags on.

- Request time to consult a third party.

- Don't let today's customer waste time to take you close to your deadline.

- Make sure you and today's customer have invested time and effort in the negotiation. If they ask you to do all the work they may not respect your efforts, and they can easily dismiss them and walk away from the negotiation. A negotiation with WOW must be collaborative.

- If today's customer pushes for a quick agreement, it may be a sign that you offered them too much value. You must slow down and reassess the value you may have conceded.

- If the negotiation is for a complex contract you should put set break times in the day to evaluate your information, and access any resources you may need.

- Request time to sleep on the consequences of an agreement if it requires a big decision.

"Let us never negotiate out of fear. But let us never fear to negotiate."

John F. Kennedy

Dirty Tricks

Trust is essential in business, but I also know that you would be foolish not to prepare for the dirty tricks used by some people. You may find yourself being tested with a series of dirty tricks to unsettle you. You don't have to be confrontational. Allow soft resilience to be your guiding light because these tricks can be easily diminished or destroyed. The following are some examples of dirty tricks in a negotiation.

- ☐ They bind a concession to an unrealistic time. Insist on adequate time: if you take on a challenge you can't handle your reputation will suffer.

- ☐ They aggressively tell you that they've got a price or a condition that they'll not negotiate on. You may decide to remove something from the negotiation too.

- ☐ They arrive late to upset your rhythm. Never let them see that you're bothered.

- ☐ They sit on a higher chair to create a feeling of superiority. Stand up or get a higher chair if it bothers you.

- ☐ They have a partner to help them create a good cop - bad cop routine. A great salesperson can adapt to different personalities. Never get complacent or feel intimidated. Deal with the facts of the negotiation.

- ☐ They try to mislead or confuse you with their terms and conditions. Make sure that there can be only one meaning for a word or term in an agreement.

- ☐ Their body language is negative for every suggestion you make. Don't base your reply on their body language. Wait until you hear their thoughts.

- ☐ They send every problem back to you because they don't want to take responsibility. You should try and accommodate them, or send a problem back and let them be more creative.

- ☐ They make a big request and follow it with a small request knowing that you may look unreasonable if you reject the small one. Take the small request and discuss it on its own merit without any influence from the big request.

- ☐ They pretend not to be interested. You must be prepared to walk away at this stage if you feel you're wasting your time.

- ☐ They try to sneak in a last concession after you've agreed terms. Make sure you receive a trade-off for the latecomer.

- ☐ They avoid giving you a direct answer. Repeat your question or rephrase it until you get your answer.

- ☐ They avoid giving you specifics and evidence. Repeat the question or rephrase it until you get an answer with the specifics and evidence.

- They offer you vague replies like, "I'll have to find that out." Get an answer as to when they expect to find that information for you.

- They arrange a phone call to suspend the negotiation and unsettle you. I wish it wasn't true, but some people have terrible egos, and they love to see other people wait on them. Stay focused with your analysis of the negotiation.

- They pretend to forget about an earlier discussion. Record and summarise your agreements as you go along. This will avoid any forgetfulness or confusion.

- They depart suddenly and try to leave you with the impression the negotiation is finished. Be polite, but never beg them to return because you'll forfeit the emotional balance of the negotiation. I'm not saying you should try to take emotion out of your communication. You shouldn't because you're dealing with human nature. Just don't over please to the extent that you lose your profit.

- They try to make you feel guilty for even negotiating. Remove the attempted manipulation by restating your selling position.

- They use evasive words like 'maybe' and 'possibly.' Don't rush to please against these words. Wait for concrete proposals and responses.

- They pretend they don't understand you in the hope that you'll forget about a request you make. Simplify and summarise your request until they understand it.

☐ They change places with a colleague during the final phase of the negotiation. This is where they hope a new dynamic will unsettle you. You must stay focused.

☐ They try to change your interpretation of the facts. Suppose I ask you, "Did you see your partner kissing your best friend?" That's different to, "Did your partner kiss your best friend?" You must take your time to dismantle every element of a question before you respond.

☐ They forecast future business from historical information. Don't allow yourself to believe the past equals the future. Align all predictions of growth to further compensation.

☐ They introduce unnecessary information to slow the negotiation down. You must question their reason for introducing the information.

☐ They ask to negotiate with another person in your company. If you agree; suspend the negotiation until the other person in your company is equipped to negotiate.

☐ They lie to you. Don't accuse them of lying. Allow them enough room to return to the truth.

☐ They try to make you feel uneasy by sitting too close to you, or by placing you in view of a sunny window. Be confident and ask for a better physical environment.

☐ They pretend the negotiation is over by gathering their documents and placing them in their briefcase. Then they relax in confident silence until you speak. Don't be intimidated by their actions or silence: communicate when you're ready to.

☐ They try to align with someone on your team, who may unintentionally turn against you. Your team must be aware of this form of manipulation. Every salesperson on your team must understand your negotiation strategy. All disagreements within your team must only be discussed in private.

☐ They take a small thing and magnify its importance before offering it as a concession. Be sure you don't get fooled into believing you've won something big when you haven't.

☐ They tell you that certain conditions can't apply in their country. You'll find that their country probably adheres to the Convention on the International Sale of Goods (CISG), the World Trade Organization (WTO), and the World Intellectual Property Organization (WIPO). Simply ask them politely for a copy of their country's law that contravenes international rules. You may find they're bluffing.

☐ They use the "Everyone wants to work with us" line to make you feel lucky to be at the negotiation table. That's not negotiation. That's a form of subtle control. If there's no mutual respect you can't create WOW.

> *"If men would consider not so much wherein they differ, as wherein they agree, there would be far less of uncharitableness and angry feeling."*
>
> **Joseph Addison**

The Agreement Fundamentals

The legally binding contract must reflect all of the verbal agreement. You need to know how you'll get paid, how much you'll get paid, and when you'll get paid. Let your legal department or your outside lawyer examine it to protect you. The following are also some things to think about.

- ☐ Put it in writing even if today's customer is your oldest friend. It's also proof you did your homework and acted professionally.

- ☐ You must understand every legal definition and its consequences.

- ☐ Check the legalese in smaller contracts that you think you can handle yourself. Here's an example. "This contract is ironclad unless you commit any of the said acts under section 9B." You may dismiss this, but what happens if one of those acts is a possibility.

- ☐ Be willing to sign as soon as possible.

- ☐ Send a letter summarising the negotiation even if you failed to reach an agreement.

- ☐ Seek ways to recover an agreement if it broke down in good faith.

- ☐ Accept why an agreement won't work if you've exhausted every possibility.

- ☐ Thank today's customer if you fail to agree, so you leave the door open for future possibilities.

Don't Kill WOW

If you're successful in your negotiation, you must never reveal what you would've settled for. That kills WOW. Your job as a negotiator is to foster cooperation for a compromise that's good for both parties. You may have got a better deal, but today's customer may have got a better deal too. If you reveal that you would've offered more or better concessions you'll only make today's customer feel bad.

HELLO PROFIT Challenge 13

Handling the Hard Negotiator

Imagine you're in a negotiation with today's customer and their mind is fixed on price, but you want to communicate a true reflection of value. Think about how you would respond to their words if you were negotiating a contract that can save your business. Think about the pressures you would face including a deadline that ends at midnight. Think about the products and services you sell, and produce a response to these statements.

- ☐ "Don't tell me your next offer if it's the same price."

- ☐ "Don't worry. I'll get it cheaper elsewhere."

- ☐ "You've one more chance to offer me a credible price."

Please remember these three very important words – respond; don't react. You must detach yourself from today's customer's possible negativity about your offer. You'll seldom experience this scenario if you follow the advice in chapters one to 12, but it pays to test yourself against a hard negotiator because it makes you sharper. This will help you increase sales, sales retention, market share, and profit. It will also improve your reputation as a salesperson who survives and thrives under extreme pressure. The best way to respond to unfair demands is to align with them and agree with today's customer. Say, "I can understand why you might feel that way. Perhaps I haven't explained myself fully. Please allow me to answer your biggest concern." This takes the sting out of the attack and removes any hint of shock and surprise in your response. It also places both of you on the moral high ground.

14. Time for Triumph

*"It is not enough to be busy.
So are the ants.
The question is;
What are we busy about?"*

Henry David Thoreau

- ☐ Precious Time
- ☐ WOW Time
- ☐ Time for Technology
- ☐ The Cost of Addiction
- ☐ Stop Playing Games
- ☐ Time for WOW
- ☐ Empire (State) Building
- ☐ Time for Transformation

- ☐ **HELLO PROFIT Challenge 14**

    Lifetime Challenge

Precious Time

You can't sell with WOW unless you protect one of life's greatest equalisers - time. No matter what you have or achieve, you only have so many hours in the day. One wasted hour in an eight hour working day can result in you losing 30 full working days a year. Let's do the maths for a five day week in a 48 week year. You'll see that the total number of hours wasted is 240. If you divide that number of hours by eight you'll get 30.

You can't afford to waste your time or today's customer's time. If you save today's customer time it adds to the value you offer them. If you waste their time you become a bigger part of their costs. That's why you must respect today's customer's time. When you waste their time you steal a part of their life, and many won't forgive you. Picture this scenario. You arranged a business meeting with today's customer, and instead of an engaging conversation of customer benefit, you wandered and waffled. The meeting could've finished in half the time with greater success if you'd been better prepared. As a result, today's customer had to play catch up and add more time to the end of their working day. This meant they left work later than planned, and they missed their daughter's bedtime story, and they were late for a romantic meal with their partner. Can you see how your inadequate preparation and poor productivity added stress to their life? Did it prove how much you disrespected them? The honest answer is 'yes'.

Think about your car, fuel, phone bills, salary, and all the other investments your company has made in you. When you understand and appreciate how much wasted time costs you and your company, you won't waste today's customer's time again.

WOW Time

Let's take an example of time wasting in the world of retail. In many supermarkets and fashion shops you may have noticed a long queue at a purchasing point. You may have also noticed average salespeople failing to spot this snake like queue filled with unhappy faces. Your face may have been one of them. Maybe these average salespeople convinced themselves that replenishing stock on the shelves, swapping gossip, and chilling out was more important than serving the people in the queue. Did you wonder if they had missed the point about today's customer being their number one priority? Did they genuinely not see the mother struggling with her children, or the business woman trying to get back to work? It's a shame that it only dawned on these average salespeople to open another purchasing point when the queue was nearly served. They killed the magic touch that may have enticed today's customer to stay longer and buy more.

Average salespeople who offer this type of uncaring service shouldn't complain when business is poor if they can't look after today's customer when their shop is full. When they leave today's customer in a queue that's unnecessary, they waste their time and the knock on effect in their life isn't good. The knock on effect from that experience isn't good for the salespeople either.

We live in a world of instant gratification. People had to walk to the shops for their newspaper years ago. Today, they can read it on their iPad or other tablet. This form of instant access creates subconscious demands in other areas of buying. There's no point saying it's not right or it's unfair. Protecting today's customer's time is a part of the WOW experience online or offline.

> "……you've got to start with the customer experience and work backwards to the technology."
>
> **Steve Jobs**

Time for Technology

Think about earliest man's discovery of the technology called fire. It was used to keep people warm, cook food, ward of predators, and light the way at night. However, some people played with fire and they got burnt. I said earlier that modern technology is essential for business today. It offers many opportunities to engage today's customer, employees, and partners more profitably, but it can hurt profit if it's underused or abused.

Every salesperson must use modern technology wisely, and move from meaningless conversations to meaningful ones that help create WOW value. Technology enables today's time-sensitive customer to choose on the move. They can evaluate products and services in seconds based on location, price, quality, availability, and service recommendations. They adore the sophistication of simplicity, so every salesperson must create sublime simplicity.

The Cost of Addiction

An average salesperson complicates the sales process with irrelevant and unfocussed conversations. That's because they're addicted to irrelevant information and stimulation, and they're anxious about being left out of the loop. They also have a need for attention. They post statements online like "Waiting for a train," or "Just had a coffee." Hi-tech is personal, but the personal element must be relevant. Wasted conversations kill time, create anxiety, and damage your career. Are your conversations valuable, or at least relevant? Are your words a broadcast about you, or a genuine desire to interact and help other people? I can understand pop stars, sports stars, movie stars, and leading business people giving an insight into their intimate moments. They've got an audience that loves to know what they ate for breakfast.

You'll find that conversations of no value contribute to a greater loss than you can imagine. Let me explain this further. I was invited to work with a senior sales manager called John. This isn't his real name for obvious reasons. John's work left him feeling overwhelmed, and he believed he was losing control of his department. His two degrees, successful career, and tactical intelligence were hampered by a dark cloud that made his role more difficult.

John wasn't overworked. He was overwhelmed by irrelevant stimulation that diluted his focus. I spent some time with John observing his diary and his communication with his team and other people. After listening and observing, I studied all of John's communication skills during two 45-minute periods. The first was between 4.15pm and 5pm one day. John believed, in that short time, he could write a short report, respond to texts, send a tweet, accept a LinkedIn request, and answer a supplier's phone call. At 5pm, I asked John if I could see his finished report, his texts and the tweet. His report had no structure and his texts and the tweet all had simple spelling mistakes. I asked him to recall his phone conversation with his supplier. He couldn't remember the supplier's full name, and he couldn't remember what he'd fully agreed to. John admitted that he hadn't listened properly to the conversation.

The second observation occurred on another day at 2pm. John had a conference phone call with colleagues in London and New York. As John spoke, I could hear his national and international colleagues tapping away furiously on their keyboards. When his colleagues spoke, John started tapping away on his laptop keyboard. When the phone call ended I asked John specific questions about his conversation with his colleagues. Sadly, my understanding of the conversation was greater than John's. Why was that so? John's tapping away on his keyboard included an email to a colleague in the building and a glance at a newspaper article online. It only took those two distractions for John to lose the essence of the conference call. John was shocked by my observations. He accepted that he'd become a victim of technology. Technology and streams of information were controlling him.

John's new understanding of communication and his intelligent use of technology allow him to be more productive and positive in his job. His team, his leader, and his family also like the results. The company now makes the most of modern technology to interact and engage, so it improves relationships and creates commercial possibilities. However, it's no longer the slave. It's the master.

It seems strange that modern technology, which is fantastic for connecting people, is also sadly responsible for distracting salespeople and confusing today's customer. It can lead to breakdowns in relationships through misunderstandings, and it can also reduce productivity and quality focused time. John now understands that he must pay attention to the intent, relevancy, timing, and emotional effect of his communication, and his need to focus on his critical challenges.

> *"Being efficient
> is not the same
> as being effective."*
>
> **Darren Kelly**

Stop Playing Games

How many apps do you have on your smartphone or tablet? How many of them clutter your screen and offer no value to your sales career? How many support you in your sales career? How many are mere distractions? Is it time to clean up your smartphone or tablet?

Apart from LinkedIn and other social media apps, let's look at 10 important types of app that can offer you support to sell with **WOW**.

☐   Driving

You need to know traffic information that includes traffic jams, accidents, diversions etc. A navigation system is a must have app to help you reach your destinations in less time.

☐   Parking

Why should you have to search for the nearest or cheapest car park? An app can save you time, stress, and money.

☐   Trains and Airplanes Scheduling

Why drive to a train station if your train has been cancelled? If you fly, why wait around an airport for your delayed flight? An app can save you time, stress, and money.

14. Time for Triumph

☐ **Recording**

Have you ever had a great idea, but you forgot it later. You need a one-touch, record and stop Dictaphone app. I suggest you use one that allows you to send the files to someone who can type them for you if you need them.

☐ **Connect to See**

There's no excuse for not being able to have an online face-to-face conversation. Skype is essential.

☐ **Sharing**

You need to be able to share files quickly. Today's customer or your colleagues may require information to make a decision. The same applies to you.

☐ **Note Taking**

If you're working on many projects you need an app to help you stay organised.

☐ **Professional Business Card Reader and Manager**

You don't have to carry other people's business cards around with you. Use an app to scan and organise your contact information for easy follow up and engagement. CamCard is a great app for this purpose.

☐ **Document Scanning**

You may need to transfer a hard copy document quickly. Why wait for your large scanner to warm up, read the document, and save it. Apps are faster and easier to use.

☐   Payment

Why wait 30, 60, or 90 days to get paid? The PayPal app or the Square app help you get paid immediately after you finish work. When you swipe today's customer's card, you get paid. It's that simple.

Time for WOW

An average salesperson will always tell me they never have enough time to achieve success. That's until I point out the obvious. I say, "You and I have 1440 minutes in a day, 168 hours in a week and 365 days in a year. That's exactly what the world's most successful salesperson has." A great salesperson treats their working time as money, and like money, they have infantry on their time. They look at the wasted unproductive hours they spend on unnecessary and irrelevant actions, and they replace them with productive and profitable actions. You must evaluate your activities and ask if they add value. Maybe some of your activities are pleasurable escapes, on the spot reactive choices, or weak and unproductive habits.

When people say they don't have the time to sell with WOW, that's untrue. What they mean to say is that they don't create time for productivity with purpose. If you don't protect your time, and if you allow clutter into your life you'll never succeed.

Empire (State) Building

A lesson in productivity with purpose can be learnt from the two men responsible for building the Empire State Building in New York. It stands proudly on the corner of Fifth Avenue and 34th Street with its 102 stories that reach 1,454 feet high. William and Paul Starrett's project management of the building was considered "an exercise in optimism" in the post Wall Street crash. Think about this for a moment. They had a plan for 2.1 million square feet of office space that had to be completed in only 13 months. They knew that if they didn't complete the building on time, the tenants who had signed up would go elsewhere, or they may have gone out of business. If the brothers had failed to complete the Empire State Building by 1st May, 1931 it would've been another disaster for an economy in turmoil.

You would be forgiven for thinking the men were slightly crazy, but you must look at how they managed their resources and time. They planned for the harsh winter of 1930 by focussing on getting the steel in place within six months. They also used slabs of pre-constructed limestone and plenty of glass to cover the building. William and Paul Starrett were famous for creating teams with chemistry that thrived on competition. The Starrets knew that time lost was money lost, but it also created discord. They eliminated their time issues by asking their employees how their lives could be made easier. Their employees suggested that food and drink for tea-breaks, and materials for building should be delivered to their work station up in the air. This made the company more productive. It proves my point that excellent communication saves time, and time saved is money saved or money earned.

Time for Transformation

Mark Twain said, "We do not deal in facts when we are contemplating ourselves." That's why it's worth keeping a WOW productivity log for a week to recognise the distractions that kill your time and affect your results. Sports stars use statistics all the time to measure their activity and their recovery from injury. A footballer can discover how fast he ran and how often. He can see how many successful passes of the ball he made, and how much possession he enjoyed.

An average salesperson hates recording a productivity log because it offers them an honest and sometimes brutal assessment. I know it's not always easy to face the truth about productivity. However, the truth will propel your career forward. This is an extreme example of wasted time, but could this be a reflection of at least one day in your career?

- ☐ 09.00. You enjoyed a coffee and a catch up with a colleague. You discussed the previous night's TV, sports game, or news.

- ☐ 09.15. You responded to several emails with no real thought.

- ☐ 09.30. You checked Facebook, or you followed someone you admired on Twitter.

- ☐ 09.40. A colleague dropped by with her thoughts about an unimportant email you sent her.

- ☐ 09.59. Your phone rang and you listened to an average salesperson.

- ☐ 10.05. You prepared for your department's weekly meeting.

- ☐ 10.10. Your phone rang. You promised to return a phone call to an unhappy customer that afternoon.

- ☐ 10.15. You accepted a LinkedIn request from an unknown person.

- ☐ 10.20. Your department meeting.

☐ 11.20. You had a meeting after the meeting to clarify some misunderstood points.

☐ 11.50. Another colleague asked, "Can I have a minute?"

☐ 13.30. You realised that this colleague didn't understand how long a minute is. You accepted the fact that he just wanted to gossip.

☐ 14.00. You called the unhappy customer back, but they were unavailable.

☐ 15.00. You arrived at a possible new customer's door to show them your company's new product.

☐ 16.15. You left your possible new customer's door. You were unsure whether they liked the product or not.

☐ 16.16. You decided to bypass the office to beat the rush hour traffic and get home early.

☐ 17.15. You arrived home with no thoughts of tomorrow's challenges.

Your challenge is to pay attention to your productivity. Some average salespeople do too many unproductive things. Other average salesperson do too little of the productive things. If you adopt the intelligence of **WOW** productivity you can enjoy more freedom, more fun, and more success. Your time and today's customer's time are precious. Don't waste them!

HELLO PROFIT Challenge 14

Lifetime Challenge

List 14 time wasters in your day. They can include

- ☐ completing unnecessary paperwork.
- ☐ enjoying a long lunch.
- ☐ poor communication.
- ☐ reading junk mail.
- ☐ waiting for answers.
- ☐ responding to unnecessary emails.
- ☐ having negative conversations.
- ☐ conflicting priorities.
- ☐ ineffective meetings.
- ☐ an unprofitable customer.
- ☐ waiting to make a perfect call at a perfect time when you know there's no such thing as a perfect time.
- ☐ skipping lunch, but having an afternoon of reduced productivity as a result

☐ meetings spaced apart when better geographical planning could've saved time and money.

☐ engaging in gossip.

When you analyse your WOW productivity log, you can decide to delegate the mildly important tasks and delete the unnecessary tasks. This removal of clutter will give you the time and clarity to create the WOW moments you need for success today.

15. Caution for Crises

*"A leader
is a dealer
in hope."*

Napoleon

☐ Crisis? What Crisis?

☐ Churchill by Your Side – 24/7

☐ Churchill and You (Tube)

☐ Churchill's Digital Victory

☐ The 9/11 British Hero

☐ Sympathy with Strength

☐ Five Words

☐ The Great News Storm

☐ Honour with Hope

☐ Fairness against Fraud

☐ People before Profit

☐ Foe to Friend

☐ **HELLO PROFIT Challenge 15**

   Crisis Debrief Challenge

Crisis? What Crisis?

A crisis is an event that causes or threatens to cause economic or physical danger and instability to people and assets in proximity. Barings Bank collapse in 1995, the Enron scandal of 2001, and Lehman Brothers bankruptcy in 2008 are examples of man-made economic crises. New York 9/11, London 7/7, and the Boston Marathon 2013 are examples of man-made criminal crises. Hurricane Katrina, Hurricane Sandy, the Indian Ocean tsunami, 2004, and Typhoon Haiyan, 2013 are examples of natural crises. The following are some of the most notable types of crises for a business.

- ❏ Flood damage can halt production in a company's property, a supplier's property, or a distributor's property.

- ❏ Faulty technology can deprive a company of the ability to do business.

- ❏ Rumours in the media about a merger, a buy-out, etc. can devalue a share price or cause employees to seek other employment.

- ❏ A strike or a minor management versus employee dispute can reduce productivity.

- ❏ A product defect that requires a recall can destroy the perception of a brand's quality.

☐   An inside fraud or violence committed by an employee can distort a company's people first image.

☐   A company's failure to pay its bills can reduce or destroy market confidence.

Other examples include hostile takeovers, customer activism, or death through negligence. When a crisis occurs, a leader must act as a company's spokesperson. Do they have to sell? Yes they do. They must grasp public concern and honestly sell corporate responsibility within a commercial context. This takes great skill. Publius Cornelius Tacitus, a former senator of the Roman Empire got it right when he said, "Reason and calm judgment: the qualities especially belonging to a leader."

I'm constantly amazed at how ill prepared many leaders are for these pivotal and politically sensitive events. Many confident and celebrated leaders have allowed calm judgement to be replaced by bluff and nervous cover up. They unknowingly suffered from *The FED Factor*™ – fear, ego, and denial. I've seen leaders smirk during crises. They may have been nervous smirks, but they never looked authoritative, respectful, or sincere. I've seen leaders squirm, fidget, avoid questions, offer insipid sound bites, and arrogantly dismiss the emotion of a crisis. They forgot that their role at that moment was to protect their company's culture and vision after paying respect to the crisis in hand. Such irresponsible behaviour can lead to full blown customer panic, economic paralysis, and a leader's departure to a career graveyard. You'll find that a leader who is emotionally intelligent will speak from their mind and heart. Their communication usually contains one or more of the following words.

☐   Alarmed

☐   Apology

- ☐ Concerned
- ☐ Cooperate
- ☐ Compensate
- ☐ Customer
- ☐ Disappointed
- ☐ Determined
- ☐ Embarrassed
- ☐ Failed
- ☐ Future
- ☐ Hope
- ☐ Happy
- ☐ Improve
- ☐ Lesson
- ☐ Promise
- ☐ Recovery
- ☐ Remedy
- ☐ Repair

- ☐ Resolve
- ☐ Saddened
- ☐ Sorry
- ☐ Sympathise
- ☐ Unhappy
- ☐ Unsatisfactory
- ☐ Victims
- ☐ Victory

> *"Anyone can hold the helm when the sea is calm."*
>
> **Publilius Syrus**

Churchill by Your Side – 24/7

Imagine having the greatest ever political communicator during a crisis, by your side. What WOW wisdom do you think Winston Churchill would offer you? Churchill, who was born on 30 November, 1874 was a twice elected British Prime Minister (1940-1945 and 1951-1955). He's famous for his leadership of Great Britain during World War Two. He was also a British Army officer, a historian, a Nobel Prize-winning writer, and a painter. John F. Kennedy said that Churchill "mobilised the English language and sent it into battle." It's no surprise that Churchill inspired New York's former mayor, Rudy

Giuliani after the 9/11 attacks. Giuliani's inspirational and aspirational words refuelled the spirit of every American when he said, "Tomorrow, New York is going to be here."

Let's take Churchill's WOW wisdom and look at it through the prism of today's 24-7 breaking news world of snapshots and sound bites.

☐ Display empathy for any victims of a crisis and their dependants. Communicate where, when, and how they can seek support.

☐ Communicate respect and understanding for any cultural or faith differences.

☐ Be honest. Never hide any dangers from your employees or stakeholders. Great Britain was immersed in World War Two during Churchill's first term as prime minister. Fluffy rhetoric to deny the truth would've been useless. The truth about any dangers to your company can inspire togetherness, and a backs-to-the wall victory. No one wants filtered and biased information. They want the truth, and that means you must suppress any natural urges you may have to sprinkle pixie dust on the truth. Because when the dust disappears, the truth will cast a spell that could destroy you and your company's credibility.

☐ Create hope to match the mood and mentality of a crisis. In 1940, the British people craved hope because hope was all they really had. A leader today must create hope and possibility before they can restore and reposition a company.

☐ Keep it simple. Warren Buffet said that simple is not easy. Churchill discovered that Abraham Lincoln memorised Shakespeare's works and the King James Version of the Bible.

Lincoln studied these works to discover words that were both noble and easily understood. It takes a lot of awareness and creativity to make things simple, but it's worth it. "We shall fight on the beaches," is better than "We shall commence battle after we engage our enemy on the coastline."

☐ Borrow from other great communicators. Was Churchill born a great speaker? The answer is 'no'. Churchill's early speeches and presentations were weak and unstructured, but he quickly learnt from the greatest ever leaders. It was his friend William Bourke Cochran (an Irish-born American lawyer, orator, and politician), who taught him how to use his voice like a musical instrument. Cochran also acted as a mentor for Franklin D. Roosevelt.

☐ Energy and passion wipe out minor flaws. No one is perfect. Churchill's speech impediment changed his "s'" into "sh's" and "zh's." Energy and passion give your words emotive power to connect with people. Perfect diction without emotion never inspires anyone.

☐ Never accept undeserved blame or divulge confidential information.

☐ Churchill said, "It is better to be making the news than taking it." You can either tell your side of the story, or you can allow traditional media and social media to tell their version of it.

☐ Fulfil your legal duties and reveal your company's on-going communication strategy.

*"Every company
is a media company."*

Darren Kelly

Churchill and You (Tube)

More people watch YouTube than TV today. That means that every leader must be able to face the cameras. These include an in house camera, a stakeholder's camera phone, or the traditional media's expert cameras. Cameras are unforgiving, so a leader must be prepared to engage, captivate, and inspire their audience. A leader can always re-record a company video, but live TV and live radio recorded on a studio webcam offer different challenges. Remember that the interviewer is focused on using your interview to break news that will inform, entertain, and increase their audience. They're trained to extract the truth. You must deliver the truth effectively and correct any inaccuracies. Make no mistake about this fact; your performance will most likely end up on YouTube for the world to see forever. Churchill would advise you to

- Study the TV or radio show, or similar style shows before you appear. Study the interviewer's personal style and be prepared for a soft and aggressive interview.

- Prepare answers to possible questions. Have your facts triple checked. Provide examples, illustrations, similarities, and contrasts to support your facts.

- Create and maintain rapport with the interviewer and your audience. Be warm and friendly, but don't relax into complacency.

- Always respond to every question.

- If you can't disclose confidential information, explain why it's confidential.

- Don't allow the interviewer to play judge and jury. The interviewer should not make statements based on bias, rumour, or misunderstanding. If the interviewer asks you about a specific subject, test their preparation too. If they ask you about certain regulations, you can ask them if they're referring to clause 2.3 in relation to clause 5.6 of a previous regulation.

- Look for ways to connect the interviewer's agenda to yours. If they ask you about developments in your industry, can you relate their questions to innovative products and services in your company? They may say, "Energy costs are rising. Today's customer is angry. What can your industry do to solve the problem?" This is a perfect opportunity for you to offer a positive answer that includes your company's plans and your industry's plans too.

- Never repeat or accept negative, loaded, or erroneous statements. For example. If they say, "You made a mess of the last speech. Where you disappointed with the reaction?" You must address both sentences. "The response to my speech was positive and the XY Times supported this fact. I'm thrilled that customer confidence was restored, and our share price rose by 23%." This is an example of where you may have to pluck your facts from your mind at a second's notice.

☐ Keep your answers short. This reduces your chances of accidentally contradicting yourself. You don't have to keep talking. Let the interviewer fill the silence.

☐ If an interviewer becomes hostile never raise your voice louder than theirs. They may be trying to provoke you. Always remain calm, warm, and in control.

☐ Drink room temperature water while waiting in the green room. No coffee or alcohol.

☐ If it's a radio show, make sure you're happy with the level of sound in your headphones. You need to hear every question clearly from the interviewer or a person phoning the show.

☐ Think about only one viewer or one listener and connect with them.

☐ Never switch off until you leave the studio and your clip on microphone is muted and removed.

☐ Make sure your clothes don't clash with the studio background. Check with the TV channel and dress in accordance with your brand and your personal comfort.

☐ Wear makeup for TV to cover any spots or blemishes.

☐ Churchill said, "The truth is incontrovertible. Malice may attack it, ignorance may deride it, but in the end, there it is." Always tell the truth. Just prepare, so your truth isn't distorted.

> "It takes 20 years to build a reputation and five minutes to ruin it. If you think about that, you'll do things differently."
>
> **Warren Buffett**

Churchill's Digital Victory

Your response to a crisis must be communicated across all available platforms. You must be able to respond to instant online conversations. You must also be aware that your communication in response to a crisis could be judged before you finish saying it. In the 2008 presidential debates in America people took time to assess their opinions before posting their messages online. In the 2012 presidential debates many people's unanalysed opinions were revealed in real time. In other words, many people responded instantly and emotionally. So here's my point. You can't shortcut your skill to deal with a crisis today. It's multi-headed, and it devours and digests information faster than ever before. There's no 'later,' and there's no 'tomorrow'. Churchill said, "A lie gets halfway around the world before the truth has a chance to get its pants on." Every lie must be nailed before it spreads. Opinion beats fact and perception usurps reality today. The best way to avoid untruths is to become a part of the online conversation before any crisis ever arises.

If a leader or a company only engages today's customer and other stakeholders during a setback or crisis they'll be seen as self-serving. If they engage them regularly, they'll most likely receive support and good will during a crisis. A perfect example of a leader who does this well is Virgin boss, Richard Branson. Branson is a master at giving his business interests a positive presence that protects him from anti-business sentiment. When he made a last-ditch bid to keep the west coast rail franchise in Britain from going to First Group in 2012, he was seen as a man defending his beliefs. If we'd never heard of Branson before, he may have appeared as a completely self-serving leader.

In 2013, Apple CEO, Tim Cook appeared before the American Senate subcommittee. They were investigating the practice of offshore profits protection from American taxes. Cook had to share Apple's side of the story in a way so that traditional media and social media would pick it up positively. He knew that most damage from an investigation is done by traditional media and social media's interpretation of what's said at such hearings. Cook made his thoughts very clear when he said, "We pay all the taxes we owe." The Huffington Post's headline read, *"Apple CEO Tim Cook To Senate Panel: 'We Pay All The Taxes We Owe."* Cook is a regular communicator with Apple's customer and stakeholder base. He has taken over from Steve Jobs with a passion to present Apple's ever evolving story. That's why he's able to use his reservoir of goodwill to protect the brand. Communication strategies like Virgin's and Apple's are no accident. They're planned very carefully.

Churchill would applaud their strategies. He said, "Failing to plan is planning to fail." I know that you're not going to please everyone all the time, but a crisis management plan that includes social media is essential. One malicious tweet can turn into a tragedy. One nasty Facebook posting can send profits plummeting. Here are some top tips to improve your chances of a crisis victory. I use the word 'victory' with reference to you and your company victoriously returning to a relationship of trust with today's customer.

- ☐ Create a crisis team that includes your best people from legal, finance, marketing, public relations, operations, and sales.

- ☐ How will your team communicate during a crisis?

- ☐ Who will draft all responses to ensure uniformity and consistency of brand values and value?

- Who will give final approval to every message?

- How will you engage in relevant conversations every day to build online trust before any possible crisis? This is not about selling products and services, but selling respect that leads to trust.

- How will you respond to any minor issues so they're never magnified or multiplied online? Is your response time online one minute, one hour, or one day?

- Does the person who manages your brand online love and know your brand? Are they social media and communication savvy?

- When you need to apologise will you post text, a video, or both?

- Who is the best person to make the video and speak in it? What location will you use? Will the sound, lighting etc. be right?

- If it's a products and services failure will you do a demonstration to remove everybody's worries?

- Who will manage negative comments on your blog or other social media sites? Do you have a series of house rules for your sites to remove illegal remarks made by internet trolls? I suggest that you never remove posts from upset people unless their words are vile or illegal. It's better to engage with upset voices if their complaints are accurate or honestly inaccurate. This will help you contain the upset and show onlookers what your brand values really are.

If Churchill held a smartphone in his hands today and he wanted to tweet a message to his audience it wouldn't read, "You ask, 'what is our aim?' I can answer in one word. It is victory; victory at all costs; victory in spite of all terror; victory, however long and hard the road may be, for without victory there is no survival." I have no doubt that if Churchill tweeted today he would type, "Our aim? - Victory at all costs; in spite of all terror; for without victory there is no survival." It's true that your possible crisis will always be different to the one Churchill experienced. However, while the context may differ, the emotions you arouse, and the responsibilities you may shoulder may feel the same. Think like Churchill in your offline or online communications. Be meaningful, be motivational, and be memorable in the moments you're needed most.

> *"Our chief want is someone who will inspire us to be what we know we could be."*
>
> **Ralph Waldo Emerson**

The 9/11 British Hero

In 2001, British born Rick Rescorla was in charge of security at Morgan Stanley Dean Witter in the World Trade Center, New York. He proved that a clearly communicated strategy can save people's lives. After the 1993 World Trade Center bombing, Rescorla believed the next attack would come from the sky. He communicated the need for the company's employees to train for a possible office evacuation. Many of the employees didn't appreciate being removed from their desks for training for an event with a low possibility of occurrence. Their initial jokes and frowns meant Rescorla had to persuade them, so they could save their own lives one day. Rescorla communicated the importance of the drill and the employees accepted his wisdom. The plan included Rescorla calling the employees to evacuate the building starting with the top floor. The employees were told to walk in pairs in case one of them needed support.

Rescorla learnt many of his formidable skills of communication during his time in British intelligence and in the US Army. As a security expert, he needed to think like a terrorist if he wished to thwart them. He also knew that after the 1993 attack, he had to think like the other employees in his company if he wished to protect them. Rescorla knew that communication is only effective if the person on the receiving end understands and appreciates a benefit.

When American Airlines Flight 11 struck the North Tower at 8.46 a.m. on the 11 September, 2001, Rescorla communicated the need for the swift evacuation of every employee from the South Tower. After United Airlines Flight 175 struck the South Tower at 9.03 a.m., Rescorla's heroism helped save the lives of 2,700 Morgan Stanley Dean Witter employees. He was last seen in the burning South Tower as he tried to save more lives. In 2009, he was remembered with the *Above & Beyond Citizen Medal*. Rescorla, who was born in Cornwall, England, was a selfless man of courage whose communication skills took WOW to a level few people ever reach.

Sympathy with Strength

A lesson in developing the human touch with WOW can be seen and heard in a speech given by the man who was known as 'The Great Communicator'. Ronald Reagan was born on 6 February, 1911. On 28 January, 1986, he put his skills to an extremely serious test. On this day, Reagan had to speak to the world and reveal that the Space Shuttle Challenger had exploded over the Atlantic Ocean. Reagan's words told the world that sadly, all seven crew members were dead. This was a major disaster on a human and technological level for America, the world's superpower.

Reagan's words wrapped comfort around his astonished audience. Many leaders try to avoid the pain of the truth. However, Reagan delivered the truth, and he gave that truth strength and hope. He paraphrased the words of a poem called *High Flight* to pay homage to those dearly loved and departed. He said, "We will never forget them, nor the last time we saw them this morning as they prepared for their journey and waved goodbye and slipped the surly bonds of earth to touch the face of God." Reagan, in that moment, helped people understand what happened. He showed that people want and deserve the truth. Many people say communicating was easy for Reagan because he was a former Hollywood actor. They forget that he spent eight years as a spokesperson for General Electric before he entered politics. It was here that he honed his skills of communication, and he learnt how to relate to and connect with any audience he ever faced. Reagan, like Churchill, like Obama, and everyone in this book wasn't a natural. He learnt how to sell with WOW.

Five Words

Barack Obama also faced a tragic test after the massacre at Sandy Hook Elementary school in Newtown, Connecticut, in 2012. An emotional Obama wiped away his tears as he reflected how every parent felt about the tragic news. A gunman entered the school and killed 27 people, including 20 children. Obama showed himself and his wife Michelle as parents. He knew, despite the horrors and pain every parent felt, the event was a stark reminder that a loving family must remind itself of its love. He inspired every parent to hug their children tight and to "remind each other how deeply we love one another." His composure faltered at times as he reminded the world that these innocent young children would never enjoy birthdays, graduations, and weddings. These five words summed up the mood of the world; "Our hearts are broken today." He ended on what was a thoughtful offering of possible hope and comfort during a devastating day. "May God bless the memory of the victims and, in the words of scripture, heal the broken-hearted and bind up their wounds."

> *"Adversity has ever been considered the state in which a man most easily becomes acquainted with himself."*
>
> Samuel Johnson

The Great News Storm

One leader who impressed me a lot in 2013 is the Vodaphone CEO, Vittorio Colao. The Italian born former McKinsey man negotiated the $130bn (£84bn) sale of Vodafone's 45 per cent stake in Verizon Wireless. I mentioned trust as an important part of business throughout the book, but Colao takes trust to another level. Verizon Communications Chairman and CEO, Lowell McAdam shares a love of cycling with Colao, and their friendship helped them negotiate the sale. Colao's interviews in the worldwide media after the sale was announced showed every leader how even great news can generate negativity. It's important that a leader remains calm and communicates the truth.

☐ Vodaphone was accused of aggressive tax avoidance. Colao responded that Vodaphone adhered to standard practices and that £54bn would be paid to Vodaphone's shareholders: many millions of them were British taxpayers. Caolo's replies managed to defend Vodaphone, explain the value to shareholders, and promote the image of additional revenue for the British tax system.

❑ Colao offered a mix of Steve Jobs promotion and Barack Obama calmness in his positive and accurate responses. He described the sale as the beginning of chapter three for Vodaphone. Chapter one was the creation of Vodaphone. Chapter two was the entering into emerging markets. Chapter three was the full digital and data phase. His forward thinking conversation about strategy was supported by words such as 'strong' and 'competent'.

❑ Colao challenged another assumption that Vodaphone would go on a buying spree. He said he didn't believe in buying sprees, but he pointed out that Vodaphone had earmarked £6 billion for investment into 4G. This message pleased Vodaphone's employees, customer base, and its shareholders.

This incident proved that great news for a leader is not always applauded. A leader must be able to peel away layers of untruth and position, package and promote a truthful message that will inspire trust and respect. Vodaphone's share prices rose after the announcement of the sale. However, Colao's ability to sell with WOW and his statement that he was "super committed" to Vodaphone's next chapter also played a part in that rise in share price.

Honour with Hope

One man showed us how the power of words can accelerate the healing process during a tragedy. Martin Luther King was born on 15 January, 1929. Like his father and grandfather before him, he became a Baptist minister. He received his PhD from Boston University when he was 26, and he became a student of Gandhi's belief in non-violent passive resistance. King noted Gandhi's speech in 1942 to The All India Congress Committee in India. The speech is known as the *Quit India* speech. Gandhi revealed that as he approached his biggest challenge he would "not harbour hatred against anybody." Those words were to have a profound effect on King, the future civil rights leader.

Many people quote King's, *I Have a Dream* speech as being his greatest ever speech, but the *Eulogy for the Martyred Children* in Birmingham, Alabama on 18 September, 1963 is also one of his finest. Three days earlier, the 16th Street Baptist Church in Birmingham, Alabama was bombed. Four innocent young girls were killed. Addie Mae Collins, Carole Robertson, and Cynthia Wesley were all 14; Denise McNair was only 11 years old. The eulogy is an example of how a leader can deliver tragic news, or reflect on a tragedy with utmost empathy. King denounced the tragedy, and then he quickly turned to the parents of the innocent girls and used his words to place the girls into the best seats in heaven. He spoke about the girls leaving this earth from a church and not a den.

King paraphrased Shakespeare's Horatio as he stood over the dead body of Hamlet. When King stood beside the coffins of the beautiful and innocent victims, he whispered good night to the "sweet princesses." His words embraced and comforted the families who were suffering their deepest grief. He used his love and compassion that seemed to come, not just from him being a preacher, but from being a loving parent too. He proved that a leader's words must sell hope with WOW. It can be their greatest gift.

Fairness against Fraud

This is the kind of story that offers a leader a significant challenge. In 1993, a man in America claimed he'd discovered a used syringe in a can of Pepsi. He said he noticed the syringe as he emptied the final contents of the can into his sink. Other people came forward within a week to make similar claims. Craig E. Weatherup was the leader of Pepsi-Cola in America at the time. Weatherup provided a lesson for any leader, who faces a crisis born out of malice. First: he ensured every Pepsi employee was kept up to date with the strategy being executed by the crisis team of four people. Second: he allowed the media to look inside the company, so he could show the world how Pepsi was canned. With the help of the FDA (Food and Drug Administration), Weatherup proved that it was impossible for a syringe to enter a Pepsi can.

Weatherup decided to be proactive with the media, and he appeared on high profile shows like Larry King Live. He also decided to place full-page ads in over 200 newspapers to reassure everyone that the Pepsi brand was safe to enjoy. When a company faces a sudden and unexpected crisis, it's only natural for its leader to feel shock and a loss of control. Their focus must shift from a planned forward strategy to facilitate both a defensive and redevelopment strategy. Weatherup didn't make the mistake of offering a response that dealt only with the short-term pressures Pepsi faced. He understood the longer view, and he believed that Pepsi's customer base and other stakeholders had to be communicated to on logical and emotional levels. This WOW formula gave Pepsi the platform for an impressive rebound.

People before Profit

How would you feel if seven people died as a result of using one of your company's products? How would you respond to the news that someone maliciously laced your product with cyanide? How would you feel if your sales dropped by 90% in just three months as a result? This is what happened to Johnson & Johnson after their Tylenol product was contaminated in 1982. Johnson &

Johnson looked at their issue with human eyes instead of financial ones. Their chairman, James Burke formed a seven-member strategy team. Burke said its aims were to protect people, and save the product after that.

They recalled 31 million bottles of Tylenol. They also motivated their employees to tour America to connect with other people in the healthcare profession to rebuild the brand. They lost over $100 million, but they knew their priority was to engage people to show they cared. The return to profit was phenomenal, and Johnson & Johnson grew stronger from that year on. In 2011, The United Nations awarded Johnson & Johnson the *Humanitarian of the Year Award* for its leading role in its *Healthy Mother, Healthy Child* initiative. The court of public opinion will always be ready to pounce. Johnson & Johnson prove that it's profitable to be good.

> *"The gem cannot be polished without friction, nor man be perfected without trials."*
>
> **Danish Proverb**

Foe to Friend

On 12 September, 1960, John F. Kennedy faced criticism that a Catholic should never become America's president. He accepted an invitation from the Greater Houston Ministerial Association, a group of Protestant religious leaders, to speak on the issue. The speech was referred to as *The Religious Issue*, but Kennedy's magnificent speech persuaded America that religion should never be an issue at all. Let's focus on how Kennedy dismantled his critics' argument that his presidency would be disastrous for America. Kennedy gave a speech that rightly receives the honour of WOW.

His main aims in the speech were to

☐ rewrite the negative headline.

☐ show that the next victim of such prejudice could be in the audience.

☐ find a common ground with the audience.

☐ defend his beliefs.

☐ be respectful and inspiring.

When Kennedy said, "I am not the Catholic candidate for president. I am the Democratic Party's candidate for president, who happens also to be a Catholic," he rewrote the headline and took control of the debate. A master communicator adopts a judo-like response by using the force of an attack to win a battle. It's a very direct approach, but it allows them to challenge what's being said without appearing upset or angry. Kennedy showed us that rapport with an audience is best achieved when you show how much you're like them too. This can be done by highlighting a shared enemy and finding an event or issue that binds you together. Kennedy pointed out that while it may have been a Catholic under the microscope of suspicion in 1960, it could be any other religion from a Jew to a Baptist another time.

Kennedy revealed the shared history of Irish people and Texans at one of Texas' most famous historical sites. He referred to the fight for the Constitution, the Bill of Rights, and the Virginia Statute of Religious Freedom with reference to the Alamo. He carefully pointed out that the Irish names McCafferty, Bailey, and Carey fought and died alongside Bowie and Crockett. Kennedy refused to pander to his critics or belittle his faith. He showed that a direct speech should not be a sermon or a lecture. It may be forceful, but it can also be humble and inspirational.

Kennedy said that defeat would be acceptable if he was judged on the issues that mattered. He understood that a direct speech with charisma, conviction, and counsel should always end with a benefit for the audience. He said that if he won the election he would devote his life to the job to "the best of my ability." The speech was a crucial turning point in Kennedy's campaign. His words of WOW took him to The White House.

HELLO PROFIT Challenge 15

Crisis Debrief Challenge

In 2013, Boston Police Commissioner Ed Davis said the Boston Marathon bombing was the "most complex crime scene in the history of our department." This proves that every crisis has many unknowns. It also highlights the importance of learning from every crisis. I hope you never experience a major crisis, let alone have to deal with a crisis similar to the one that pierced the world's heart on 15th April, 2013. I also hope you learn from every mini or major crisis you face. Your crisis debrief may protect you in the future.

- ☐ How long did it take for your team to discover the crisis?

- ☐ How long did it take for your team to discover the traditional media and social media's comments about it?

- ☐ What was the response time?
- ☐ Was the communication response accepted and acted upon?
- ☐ Did you rebuild trust?
- ☐ Did you respect the ethics of your brand values?
- ☐ How was your communication perceived by those people not directly affected?
- ☐ Did everyone act as planned?
- ☐ How can you make sure any mistakes will never be repeated?
- ☐ Could the crisis have been avoided? How?
- ☐ Who needs ongoing support?
- ☐ How can you support them?

If you don't like the answers you receive ask

- ☐ Why?
- ☐ Is there a better way?
- ☐ Churchill said, "A nation that forgets its past has no future." A company must learn fast, and create a better way to deal with its next possible crisis.

WOW Forever

*"No space of regret
can make amends
for one life's opportunity
misused."*

Charles Dickens

- Three Wise Salesmen
- Dickens Today
- Prime Selling

Three Wise Salesmen

In 1844, Charles Dickens was overjoyed upon hearing the news that 6,000 copies of *A Christmas Carol* had been sold on the day of its publication. Was Dickens a great salesperson who sold with WOW? Yes, he was. In fact, he's the father of selling with WOW. In the story, Dickens' ghosts framed, positioned, and explained Scrooge's predicament in a very compelling way that still astounds the marketing giants on Madison Avenue.

The Ghost of Christmas Past sold Scrooge the idea that his misery was predominantly related to his previous decisions. *The Ghost of Christmas Present* sold Scrooge the idea that he had to help solve the problems of people who were less fortunate. *The Ghost of Christmas Yet to Come* sold Scrooge the idea that change is possible. When Scrooge asked the third ghost to erase the writing on his own headstone he was asking for a chance to remove his shame and embrace true happiness. After the ghostly visits, Scrooge became a great salesperson too. A remorseful Scrooge sold himself the idea that he had to change immediately. He didn't say, "I know what to do, but I'll wait until next Monday or next year." He ordered a turkey for Bob Cratchit's family, and he raced to his nephew Fred's party at a speed that would impress Usain Bolt.

Every Christmas when I read *A Christmas Carol* I smile when Scrooge pulls back the curtains. "No fog, no mist; clear, bright, jovial, stirring, cold; cold, piping for the blood to dance to; Golden sunlight; Heavenly sky; sweet fresh air; merry bells. Oh, glorious! Glorious!" Dickens' story of social justice brought generosity of wealth and spirit to the world.

It helped shape modern Christmas into a season of success filled with salvation, reconciliation, and celebration. Aren't we lucky that Dickens understood the power of selling with WOW? Aren't we lucky that he sold his story with WOW? So how did he do it?

Dickens insisted the story's price was fixed at five shillings to achieve higher sales. He sold space for advertisements in his original serialised books. Dickens also gave numerous speeches to audiences of up to 4,000 people at a time to promote his work. Dickens, in many ways, was a 19th century Steve Jobs. He believed in his work so much that he wanted to share it with the world. He knew he could only do that by selling it with WOW.

Dickens Today

I look at some modern leaders, and I wonder if they learnt the same selling lessons from Dickens. When Ralf Speth, the CEO of Jaguar Land Rover appeared on SKY News (Britain) in 2012 to speak about Jaguar's launch of the New F-Type Sports Car, he said it was an exciting day for Jaguar. Was his appearance an opportunity to sell the car and the brand? You bet it was. Karren Brady is one of Britain's most famous and respected businesspeople. The Vice-Chairman of West Ham United is also Lord Sugar's right-hand person on *The Apprentice*. In her honest and inspiring book *Strong Woman* she sells the idea that ambition is an admirable thing. Brady's advice has helped many women rediscover their self-belief and discover their hidden promise. In Sheryl Sandberg's brilliant book, *Lean In*, the Facebook CEO also sells the idea of a better life for every ambitious young woman in business.

When Yahoo CEO, Marissa Meyer gave her first live interview to Patti Sellers of *Fortune* magazine she sold the idea of Yahoo being an innovative and caring company – one that simplified the customer experience in the real world. She also sold the idea that her passion for Yahoo was on a Super Bowl winning level. Meyer spoke about the inspiration she learned from former Green Bay Packers' coach, Vince Lombardi, the man whose name graces the Super Bowl trophy. Lombardi once described his priorities as "God, family, and the Green Bay Packers." Meyer repeated the quote, but she replaced "the Green Bay Packers" with "Yahoo."

How about Qualcomm's Paul Jacobs' charismatic performance at the Consumer Electronics show in 2013 in Las Vegas? When he spoke about micro technology in our blood streams that can warn us of an imminent heart attack, did he sell Qualcomm's value to the world? I think so. What about Rich Teerlink, the former CEO of Harley Davidson? Dickens would've admired how he sold Wall Street and the world on the vision that Harley Davidson didn't make motorbikes. He repeated that they created an experience for the person who wanted to feel cool. He said, "What we sell is the ability for a 43 year old accountant to dress in black leather, ride through small towns and have people be afraid of him." Wall Street responded with a sharp rise in the company's share price. Teerlink's words of WOW earned his company a fortune.

> "The people who get on in this world are the people who get up and look for the circumstances they want, and, if they can't find them, make them."
>
> **George Bernard Shaw**

Prime Selling

What about Amazon's Jeff Bezos, who announced that Amazon was testing delivery by unmanned drones? The octocopters can deliver a paperback version of *HELLO PROFIT* to your front door within 30 minutes. Bezos' words created a WOW moment on the eve of Cyber Monday, 2 December, 2013. The service, called *Prime Air,* has some critics suggesting it was just a prime time stunt for maximum publicity. One thing is for sure: Amazon and WOW were mentioned in the same sentence in the global media. I'm sure Dickens would've agreed that such promotion can only be great for sales and profit.

The end

P.S. I'd love to know your views on HELLO PROFIT. What have you learnt? What elements of the book work best for you? How has it changed your life? What did you most enjoy most about the book? Which nugget of selling and customer service gold will you share with your colleagues? Please email support@darrenkelly.tv

Are You a Sales Leader in B2B?

☐ Is your industry competitive?

☐ Have you 8 or more people on your team?

☐ Do they phone people or meet them face-to-face?

☐ Do you expect more from them?

☐ Would you like your team to benefit from effective face-to-face or online coaching to upgrade their sales skills?

Please email support@darrenkelly.tv

My team and I offer the ultimate blueprint for developing you and your company's own authentic communication style.

HELLO PROFIT Workbook and 6 CDs

Solutions for a better Sales Strategy Today

WORKBOOK includes

- ☐ WOW email templates
- ☐ WOW marketing words 'plus'
- ☐ WOW Negotiation 'plus'
- ☐ WOW Creativity
- ☐ WOW Success principles 'plus'
- ☐ And much more WOW

The 6CDs include a unique delivery of the book with extra value material and 'strategic insights plus' to increase your sales today. Visit darrenkelly.tv

HELLO PROFIT Mobile Course

Sometimes it's hard to access a mentor when you need them most. Let me be your mentor 24 hours a day.

- ☐   Ideal for anyone with a small business or anyone who wants to make it big in business.

- ☐   The ultimate key to greater sales now, tomorrow, or anytime and anywhere on your desktop, tablet, or smartphone.

- ☐   Includes never before discussed insights into the biggest sales in history.

Visit darrenkelly.tv

DO YOU KNOW

someone who needs to hear a similar message of motivation and empowering communication that's in HELLO PROFIT? If they prefer to read a similar message in fiction please gift them

Happy Now Happy Forever by Darren Kelly.

The book includes 10 inspiring conversations I had with Betty Ford (Vitality), Yves Saint Laurent (Confidence), Frederick Douglass (Freedom), Coco Chanel (Abundance), Rosa Parks (Equality), Evelyn Lauder (Love), Mary Anderson (Purpose), Martin Luther King (Hope), Marie Curie (Time), and Neil Armstrong (Patience). Each fictional conversation occurred on their last day alive.

They prove that despite constant technological evolutions, the same emotions, instincts, and intellects that drove human behaviour on day one, also drive your behaviour today. My hope is that the conversations offer you a moment of reflection to illuminate and empower your life and the lives of those you touch – now and forever.

Extra Sources and Further Reading

Every person in this book has been observed and studied over long periods of time. The list below represents a small section of my research and observations.

Part I

1. Gratitude for Growth

- Oprah Winfrey The Definitive Story of Her Struggle and Success by George Mair

- The Oprah Winfrey Show (final)

- The Oprah Winfrey Show: Reflections on an American by Deborah Davis

- http://www.oprah.com/index.html

- http://entertainment.time.com/2013/06/26/women-lead-list-of-most-powerful-celebrities/

- Pour Your Heart into it by Howard Schultz

- 007: licensed to place product – The Guardian 2 April 2012

2. Values for Victory

- Swoosh: The Unauthorized Story of Nike and the Men Who Played There by J.B. Strasser

- Nike (Corporations That Changed the World) by Tracy Carbasho

- Bowerman and the Men of Oregon: The Story of Oregon's Legendary Coach and Nike's Cofounder by Kenny Moore

- Nike Culture: The Sign of the Swoosh (Cultural Icons series) by Robert Goldman and Stephen Papson

- http://nikeinc.com/pages/executives

- http://www.time.com/time/magazine/article/0,9171,996843,00.html

3. Energy for Excellence

- Think BIG: Make it happen in business and life by Donald Trump

- The Art of the Deal by Donald Trump

- Never Give Up: How I Turned My Biggest Challenges into Success by Donald Trump

- How to Get Rich by Donald Trump

- http://www.trump.com/Donald_J_Trump/Donald_J_Trump.asp

- http://www.time.com/time/magazine/article/0,9171,956733,00.html

4. Listening for Luck

- Grinding It Out: The Making Of McDonald's by Ray Kroc
- Forbes Greatest Business Stories of All Time: 20 Inspiring Tales of Entrepreneurs Who Changed the Way We Live and Do Business by Forbes magazine Staff and Daniel Gross
- Biography: Ray Kroc (DVD)
- McDonalds: behind the Arches by John F. Love
- http://www.mcdonalds.com/us/en/our_story/our_history/the_ray_kroc_story.html
- http://www.time.com/time/magazine/article/0,9171,989785,00.html

5. Sharing for Success & 6. Network for Net Worth

- Reverse Innovation: Create Far From Home, Win Everywhere by Vijay Govindarajan and Chris Trimble
- Pepsi: 100 Years by Bob Stoddard
- Indra Nooyi is Pepsi chairman Feb 6, 2007 http://articles.timesofindia.indiatimes.com/2007-02-06/

- india-business/27879841_1_indra-nooyi-steven-reinemund-executive-chairman

- http://www.pepsico.com/Company/Leadership.html

- http://www.businessweek.com/magazine/indra-nooyi-rediscovers-the-joy-of-pepsi-02022012.html

- http://live.wsj.com/video/pepsi-indra-nooyi-on-balancing-work-and-family/44313778-BE51-4C1A-9323-8757ED876F78.html#!44313778-BE51-4C1A-9323-8757ED876F78

- Pepsi chief pursues snack innovation - FT July 18, 2013

- The Start-up of You: Adapt to the Future, Invest in Yourself, and Transform Your Career -Reid Hoffman and Ben Casnocha

- http://www.time.com/time/magazine/article/0,9171,1229207,00.html

Part 2.

7. Belief for Brilliance

- The Road Ahead by Bill Gates

- Gates: How Microsoft's Mogul Reinvented an Industry-- and Made Himself the Richest Man in America by Stephen Manes

- ☐ Impatient Optimist: Bill Gates in His Own Words by Bill Gates and Lisa Rogak

- ☐ The Success Secrets Of Bill Gates: The Inspirational Story And Success Secrets Of Microsoft Billionaire Bill Gatesby Anthony Taylor

- ☐ Hard Drive: Bill Gates and the Making of the Microsoft Empire by J Wallace

- ☐ Business at the Speed of Thought: Succeeding in the Digital Economy by Bill Gates

- ☐ http://www.microsoft.com/en-us/news/exec/billg/

- ☐ http://www.time.com/time/photogallery/0,29307,1630529,00.html

8. Rapport for Relationships

- ☐ Made in America My Story by Sam Walton

- ☐ The Unwinding - George Packer

- ☐ Mr. Sam: How Sam Walton Built Wal-Mart and Became America's Richest Man by Karen Blumenthal

- ☐ The Amazing Sam Walton: (Success of Wal-Mart) by Therlee Gipson

- ☐ How & Why Sam Walton Invented Wal-Mart by Vance Trimble

- The Wal-Mart Decade: How a New Generation of Leaders Turned Sam Walton's Legacy by Robert Slater
- http://corporate.walmart.com/our-story/heritage/history-timeline
- http://business.time.com/2012/07/02/ten-ways-walmart-changed-the-world/

9. Wisdom for Winning

- Made in Japan: Akio Morita and Sony by Akio Morita
- How They Started: Global Brands: How 21 good ideas became great global businesses by David Lester
- Sony: The Private Life by John Nathan
- http://www.sony-europe.com/article/id/1178278971500
- http://www.time.com/time/world/article/0,8599,2054745,00.html

10. Passion for Promotion

- Steve Jobs: The Exclusive Biography by Walter Isaacson
- Steve Jobs The Man Who Thought Different by Karen Blumenthal
- The Apple Revolution: Steve Jobs, the counterculture and how the crazy ones took over the world by Luke Dormehl

- ☐ I, Steve: Steve Jobs in His Own Words by George Beahm
- ☐ Steve Jobs: Ten Lessons in Leadership by Michael Essany
- ☐ The Steve Jobs Way: iLeadership for a New Generation by Jay Elliot
- ☐ Return to the Little Kingdom: Steve Jobs, the creation of Apple, and how it changed the world by Michael Moritz
- ☐ http://www.apple.com/uk/stevejobs/
- ☐ http://www.time.com/time/magazine/article/0,9171,986849,00.html

11. Habit for Harmony

- ☐ Estee a Success Story: A Success Story by Estee Lauder
- ☐ Estee Lauder: Beyond the Magic by Lee Israel
- ☐ http://www.time.com/time/specials/packages/article/0,28804,2029774_2029776_2031810,00.html
- ☐ Estee Lauder: Businesswoman and Cosmetics Pioneer: Businesswoman and Cosmetics Pioneer by Robert Grayson
- ☐ Make-up maker sees moderate economic growth by FT on YouTube
- ☐ http://www.elcompanies.com/Pages/Our-History.aspx

Part 3.

12. Asking for Agreement

13. Nerve for Negotiation

- ☐ Secrets Of Power Negotiating : 15th Anniversary Edition Inside Secrets From a Master Negotiator by Roger Dawson

- ☐ Secrets of Power Negotiating for Salespeople: Inside Secrets from a Master Negotiator by Roger Dawson

- ☐ Negotiation Genius: How to Overcome Obstacles and Achieve Brilliant Results at the Bargaining Table and Beyond by Deepak Malhotra and Max Bazerman

- ☐ Negotiation: The Brian Tracy Success Library by Brian Tracy

14. Time for Triumph

- ☐ Sky Boys: How They Built the Empire State Building by Deborah Hopkinson by James E. Ransome

- ☐ Empire State Building (Wonders of the World) by Elizabeth Mann

15. Caution for Crises

- ☐ http://uschs.wordpress.com/tag/william-bourke-cochran/

- [ ] Pepsi Punches back with PR blitz by The Washington Post 19 June 1993

- [ ] When the Bubble Burst by The Economist 3 August 1991

- [ ] http://allthingsd.com/tag/dick-costolo/

- [ ] Tylenol and the Legacy of J&J's James Burke – Time - 5, October 2012

- [ ] The Greatest Speeches of President John F. Kennedy by John F. Kennedy

- [ ] The Bay of Pigs (Pivotal Moments in American History) by Howard Jones

- [ ] Boston Marathon bombs: April 16 as it happened by The Telegraph

WOW Forever

- [ ] Charles Dickens as I Knew Him: The Story of the Reading Tours in Great Britain and America (1866-1870) by George Dolby

- [ ] Life of Charles Dickens by Frank Thomas Marzials

- [ ] The Life of Charles Dickens: Volume 2. 1842-1852 by John Forster

- [ ] Dickens by Adolphus William Ward

Special Acknowledgements

With love to Eleanor, Martha, Harriet, and Elizabeth

I must pass credit on to the great minds who inspired this book. These people have a service attitude that's built on gratitude, great values, energy, a listening mind, and a desire to connect. I also admire their confidence, empathy, thirst for knowledge, passion to inspire, and respect for consistency.

- Lord Kirkham. What did I do to deserve your wisdom and inspiration? Thank you for cutting my learning curve by at least two years. Your inspiration and subtle motivation helped me create this book. "Hello" sums up your warmth and passion, and "Profit" sums up your skill to serve and support.

- Donald J. Trump. Thank you for inspiring me with WOW and for taking the time to read *HELLO PROFIT*.

- Dermot Desmond. You prove that success never changes you. It only highlights who you really are. Thank you for your inspiration and kindness.

- Michelle Mone - the Bra Queen. Thank you for your insights into innovation, success, and the power of personal and business honesty.

- Lawrence Tomlinson. Every time we meet I learn something extremely valuable; not just for business, but for life.

- ☐ Brian Tracy. You're not only the greatest sales trainer in the world. You're a wonderful human being.

- ☐ Meredith McIver. Thank you for your inspiration.

- ☐ The team at Createspace. You are true artists and great people.

- ☐ Roger Dawson. You're a mentor who supports, inspires, and truly cares.

- ☐ Wayne Allwine – the voice of Mickey Mouse for 22 years. RIP. You taught me the essence of customer service in our short time together. It wasn't just the Disney way; it was the only way.

- ☐ Al Ries. You're the world's number one marketing man. I've learnt so much from you as a marketer, but more importantly as a person.

- ☐ Sarah Day. You have the rare ability to let your immense leadership talent and skill shine through your humility. Thank you for inspiring me.

- ☐ Dominic De Luca. My great friend. You always say, "First and foremost. The customer comes first."

- ☐ Leo Hemmings – one of life's greatest givers – a model of greatness and charity.

- ☐ Jon Hammond - a positive voice for success and life.

- ☐ Angie Zambrano for 3D imaging.

☐   Bob Charlton, Sandy Needham, Russ Piper, Caroline Cundey, Paul Caplan, John Tague, Mel Schwartz, Stephen Kenny, Paul Holohan, Alan Weiss, Kirstie Allerton, Geoff Shepherd, John Taylor, Alan Carruthers, Carl Emms, Alan Weiss, Darren Owers, Eamonn Holmes, Tim Bailey, Steven Gash, Alyson Wort, Michael Eisner, Paul Mackie, Andrew Edwards, Don Rooker, James Somerville, Cher, Pat Garvey, Jill Konrath, Sarah Whittaker, Anthony McCann, Jim Bourne, John Tordoff, Malcolm Gladwell, Dave Lyons, David Byrne, Bernard Ginns, and Eleanor Mills.

I'm forever grateful to you all.

Copyright & Conditions

With the exclusion of short quotations for review, reproduction or deployment is prohibited, unless advance written permission has been received from the author. The use of this material in seminars, workshops and other training programmes is also prohibited, unless advance written permission has been received from the author.

This material is for information purposes only, and the publisher and the author don't guarantee that it will be suitable for your personal and/or professional circumstances. Please consult your lawyer, accountant, doctor, psychologist, psychotherapist, or other professional experts before you adopt any of the ideas in the book. The author and the publisher also can't be liable to you or anyone else for any exclusion or error or for any damages that result. The publisher and the author won't be liable for any damages that result from any inability to use or the complete use of the information. References to trademarks are used in accordance with the Fair Use Doctrine. They don't suggest that this book is a vehicle to advertise them. Any errors will be rectified in future editions.

Index

A
A World Champion Hello, 97
Activate Self-belief, 122
Addiction (Time), 264
Advertising Age, 37
Agreement Fundamentals, The, 256
Ahrendts, Angela, 42
American Spectator, The, 56
Answers (rapport), 162
Apple, XXII, XXIII, XXXI, 43, 108, 165, 187, 189, 190, 191, 192, 193, 196, 198, 200, 287
Apple II, 187
Apple Presentation (WOW – An), 189
Apps, 266
Armstrong, Lance, 153
Art of WOW, The, xxi
Ash, Mary Kay, xxx,

Ask after Rejection, 237
Ask for Yes, 233
Ask with Obligation, 230
Ask with Trust, 232
Ask with WOW, 236
Ask without Fear, 235
Aviator, xxxvii
Avoid a Concrete Culture, 84

B
Barbie, 6
Basket Case to Brilliance, 10
Be a Twit, 111
Belief to Communicate, 129
Best Served Cold, 92
Better Asking, 237
Bezos, Jeff, xxxi, 27, 28, 58, 193, 305, 306
Bill and Melinda Gates Foundation, The, 126
Blakely, Sarah, xxxi, 28

BMW, xxvi
Body Language Secrets, 48
Bolt, Usain, 46
Boston Marathon, 298
Boston University, 293
Brady, Karren, xxxi, 304
Bra-llelujah, 54
Branson, Richard, xxxi, 92, 175, 286, 287
Breaking Bad, 179
Breath of Success, 56
Bush senior, George, 154
Business Week, 27

C
Carlyle, Thomas, 50
Celtic Football Club, 10
Cher, 147
Churchill and You (Tube), 283
Churchill by your Side 24/7, 280
Churchill, Winston 65, 77
Churchill's Digital Victory, 286
Circles of Strength, 220
CISG, 255
Citibank, 10, 127
Clooney, George xxiv
Closing, 229
CNN, 13
Cochrane, Johnny, xxiv
Coke xxii, xxiii, xxvi, 5
Colao, Vittorio 292, 293
Commerzbank, 11
Company Gratitude, 10

Concessions, How to Offer, 248
Connect the World, 186
Connors, Carol, 200
Control Your Energy, 51
Cook, Tim, 191, 287
Crisis Debrief Challenge, 398
Crisis? What crisis?, 277
CRM, 81
Cruise, Tom, xxiv
Customer Gratitude, 11

D
Decisions of Destiny, 28
Definitive Book of Body Language, The, 48
Desmond, Dermot, xxxi, 10
Dickens Today, 304
Dickens, Charles, 301, 303, 304, 305
Digicel, 13
Dior, Christian, 41
Dirty Tricks, 251
Disney, Walt, 198
Does the Child Rule, 126
Don't Close, 229
Don't Kill WOW, 257
Dyson, 13

E
Edison, Thomas, 9, 232
Einstein, Albert, 25, 132
Elizabeth 2, Queen, 16,
Eloquence of Easy, The, 191

Email, Engage with, 113
Emerson, Ralph Waldo, 17, 70, 95
Empathy (Rapport), 161
Empire (State) Building, 268
Energy Booster, 59
Energy for Giving Back, 46
Energy Rebooted, 53
Energy to Compete, 43
Ernst and Young, 13
Everlasting Story, The, 197
Evil Enemy, The, 191
Exciting Feeling, The, 194
Eyes of WOW, 148

F
Facebook, xxxii, xxx, 43, 270, 287, 304
FED Factor, The, 278
FedEx, xxvii
Ferguson, Sir Alex, 45, 215
50 Cent, 5
Financial Services Centre Dublin, 10
Find Your WOW Mentor, 172
First Lady of WOW, The, 208
Fischer, Bobby, 57
Five Words, 291
5% Principle, The, 140,
Flight Plan, 67
Foe to Friend, 296
Forbes, 29, 72, 147 , 147
Ford, Henry, 6, 9
Ford, Tom, xxx
Foreman, George, xxiv
Forget Your Hot Air Balloon, 171
Fortune Global Forum, 17
Fortune Magazine, 79, 126, 152, 296, 304
Franklin Store, Ben, 148
Franklin, Benjamin, 32, 176
FTSE Group, 38

G
Galeries Lafayette, The, 219
Gates, Bill, xxxi, 28, 126, 127, 128, 140, 141
Genius Bar, 196
Get Better Now, 216
Giuliani, Rudy, 280
Glorious Vision, The, 198
Go Outdoors, 223
Goddess of Victory, 35
Golden Phone Calls, 100
Golden Phone, The, 101
Gonna Fly Now, 200
Gorgeous Goodbye, The, 201
Gratitude Generator Company, 22, 23
Gratitude Generator Customer, 24
Gratitude Generator Personal, 21, 22
Gratitude Trilogy, The, 5
Gucci, xxx

H

Habit of WOW, The, 223
Hamburger University, 69
Handler, Ruth, 5
Handling the Hard Negotiator, 257
Happy Habit, The, 223
Harley Davidson, xxxi, 305
HARPO, xxxi, 8
Harrods, 13, 19
Heineken, xxvii,
High Flyers, 6
Hoover, Herbert, 154
Huffington Post, The, 287
Humanitarian of the Year Award, 296

I

I Have a Dream, 156
Iceland Foods, 93,
Image of Energy, The, 46
Immelt, Jeff, 13
India, 20
Insanity of WOW, The, 201
Inside The Actors Studio, xxiv
Inside Todays Customer, xxviii
Inside Your Competition, xxvi
Inspirational Values, 32
International Investment & Underwriting, 10
Intimacy of WOW, The, 222
Irish Post Awards, The, 97
Isaacson, Walter, 187

iTech Guy, The, 198, 199
iTunes Store, 188

J

Jackson, Michael, 36
Jay-Z, 29
JCB, 13
Jobs, Steve, xxxi, 28, 187, 189,190,191, 192, 193, 194, 196, 197, 198, 200, 201, 203, 211, 263, 287 293, 304
Johnson & Johnson, 295, 296
Johnson, Magic, 15
Johnson, Samuel, 292
Jordan. Michael, 35
Just Do It (Right), 36

K

Kelly's Customer Compass, 133
Kelly's Lucky Message, 87
Kelly's Sales Ladder, 217
Kennedy, John F., 154, 155
Kenya, 19
Kettering, Charles F, 20, 119
Killing Success, 128
Kindle 2, 193
Kindle Fire, 58
King, Martin Luther, 65, 156, 293, 294
King, Roger, 8
Knight, Phil, xxxi, 34, 35, 36, 37, 38

Konrath, Jill, 167
Kroc, Ray, xxxi, 65, 66, 67, 68, 69, 72

L
Lauder, Estée, 216, 217, 219, 220
Laughing Matter, The, 205
Lie - The Big Fat Lie, 153
Lie - The Lie Detector, 155
Lie - The Reckless Lie, 154
Lie - The Silent Lie, 155
Lie To Me, 47
Lifetime Challenge, 272
LinkedIn, 108, 109, 110, 111, 134, 264, 266, 270
Listen to the Whole Conversation, 64
Listen Truthfully, 69
Listen Without Ego, 68
LNT Group, 90

M
Made in Japan, 178
Madoff, Bernie, 151
Martin, Ricky, 146
McCall, Carolyn, 171
McDonald's, xxxi, 21, 65, 66, 67, 68, 69, 72, 74
McGuigan, Barry, 97
Meeting Bill Again, 141
Meeting Bill, 140
Mentor Mentee Guidelines, 177
Meyer, Marissa, xxxi, 304

Michael, George, xxiii,
Microsoft, xxxi, 126, 127, 128, 205
Mone, Michelle, xxxi, 54
Morita, Akio, xxxi, 174, 175, 176, 177, 178, 179
Morrison, Denise, xxxi, 29
Morrison, Ken, 242
M-Pesa, 19

N
Negotiate With WOW, 241
Negotiation (Types of), 241
Net Worth Generator, 115
New York Times, 220
Newton, Isaac, 100
Nike, xxxi, 9, 35, 36, 37, 38
9/11 British Hero, The, 289
No Fear, 124
Nooyi, Indra, xxxi, 79, 80, 83, 86, 92, 104

O
O'Brien, Denis, 13
O2 Ireland, 112
Obama, Barack, xxii, xxiii, 16, 18, 58, 206, 207, 209, 291, 293
Obama, Michelle, 208, 209
Ohga, Norio, 177
Omega, xxvi,
One-Company, 79
One-Win Agreement, 248

Oprah, xxxi, 8, 9, 10, 28, 45, 51
Origin of Brands, The, 21
Origin of Species, The, 85
OWN Network, 8

P
Palin, Sarah, 51
Passion by Design, 186
Pease, Allan and Barbara, 48
Penney, JC, 148
Pepsi, xxxi, 79, 80, 86, 290
Personal Gratitude, 6
Pink Habit, The, 220
Plan with Ears, A, 73
Playing to Win, 242
Polgár, Klara and László, 29
Ponzi, Charles, 151
Popular Electronics, 126
Power of Punchy, The, 200
Precious Time, 261
Prime Air, 306
Prime Selling, 305
Proposals, 165, 166
PS4, 179

Q
Quaker Oats, 86
Qualcomm, 305
Questions (Rapport), 160

R
Rapport after Sales, 165
Rapport from Refusals, 164
Rapport in Meetings, 157
Rapport in Ruins, 151
Rapport to Remember, 156
Rapport with Groups, 164
Reagan, Ronald, 290
Reebok, 37
Refreshing Inspiration, 221
Reignite Your Passion, 210
Reject Rejection, 125
Remember My Name, 149
Rescorla, Rick, 289
Responsive Listening, 70
Rose, Charlie, 13
Run for Your Life, 34

S
75% Principle, The, 129
Saks, 216
Sandberg, Sheryl, 304
Sandy Hook, 291
Schiller, Philip, 192
Schultz, Howard, xxxi, 14, 15
Selfridge, Harry, 11, 12, 188
Selfridges, 11, 12
Sell with Silence, 58
Selling Position with WOW, 246
Sharapova, Maria, xxiv
Share a Coke, xxii,
Sharing with Purpose, 79
Silent Listening, 63
Simple Solution, The, 193
SKY News, 304
Skyfall, xxvi
Sleep Your Way to Success, 55

Sleepy and Dopey, 188
Smith, Will, 129
Snap Selling, 167
Sonneborn, Harry, 68
Sony Mentoring, 174
Sony, xxxi, xxvi, 174, 175, 176, 177, 178, 179
Sorrel, Martin, 18
Sound Wisdom, 174
Stanford, 34
Starrett, William and Paul, 268
Stevenson, Robert Louis, xxi
Stimulate Belief, 127
Stop Playing Games, 266
Sullenberger, Chesley 'Sully', 203
Sunday Times, 18, 93,
Super Bowl, 305
Superstar WOW, 146
Survivor, 8
Sympathy with Strength, 290

T
10TY (10 Times You), 141
30-Second Pitch, 138
3S Internal Sharing, 81
Take a Bow, 27
Talk Asia, 14
Team Player, The, 93
TED, 41, 200
Teerlink, Rich, 305
TESCO, 172
The Soldier, the President, and the Queen, 16
Three Wise Salesmen, 303

Time Dangers, 249
Time for Now, 268
Time for Technology, 263
Time for Transformation, 269
Today's Culture Club, 17
Today's Customer's Spirit, 20
Today's Global Customer, 13, 14, 15, 16, 17
Tomlinson, Lawrence, xxxi, 90
Top Gun, xxvii
Tracy, Brian, 67
Tropicana, 86
Trump Express, The, 55
Trump, Donald, xxxi, 42, 44, 45, 46, 47, 48, 49, 55, 56, 171
Trust and Value, 79
Twain, Mark, 189, 269
Twitter, xxii, 43, 111, 113, 134, 138, 191, 270

U
Ultimate Headline, The, 191
Uno, Sandiago, 6

V
Valued Call, The, 107
Values that Hurt, 38
Virgin, xxxi, 175, 286, 287
Vodaphone, 292, 293

W
Walker, Malcolm, 92
Wall Street, 305

Wal-Mart, xxxi, xxix, 147, 148, 149, 150
Weatherup, Craig E, 295
Welch, Jack, 152
What Chinese Want, 18
What Makes McDonald's?, 72
Whelan, Dave, 242
When Hands Betray, 50
When Things Go Wrong, 203
White, Walter, 179
Williams, Pharrell, 115
Wilson Sports, xxvii
WIPO, 255
Wisdom that Protects, 176
World Trade Center, 289
WOW – The Key to Success, xxi
WOW for Life, 216
WOW Listening, 71
WOW Preparation, 243
WOW Time, 262
WOW-Mart, 147
WTO, 255

X
Xerox, 15

Y
Yahoo, 304, 305
You as a WOW Mentee, 180
You as a WOW Mentor, 181
Your True Self, 123
YouTube, xxii, 7, 72, 116, 283

Z
Zuckerberg, Mark, xxx

Printed in Great Britain
by Amazon.co.uk, Ltd.,
Marston Gate.